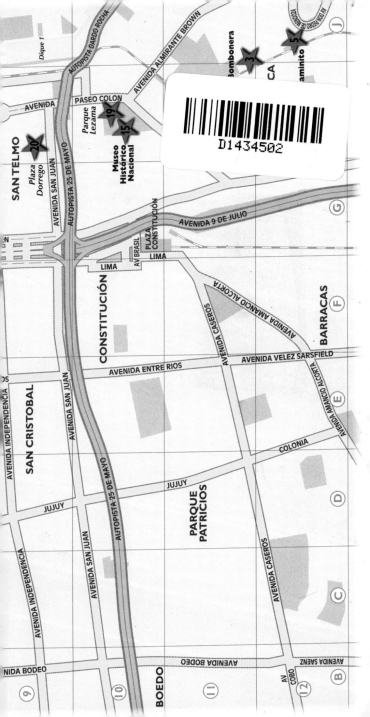

DOG WALKERS

Around the city's well-heeled *barrios* you will often see *paseaperros* (dog walkers). Busy Porteños regularly hand over their prize labradors and bassets to these muscular canine carers, who can exercise up to two dozen hounds at a time through the city's streets and parks, somehow managing to avoid tangling all the leads.

FREUD

In a city where Woody Allen is a favourite film director, it comes as no surprise to learn that, in the world, only New York has (slightly) more psychoanalysts per capita. Visits to the shrink are usually covered by private medical insurance and there are so many mental health practices in one part of Palermo (▷ 98–103) that it is known as Villa Freud.

Focus On Tango

Just as not everyone in Vienna can waltz, don't expect all Porteños to tango down the street. That said, tango is a prominent feature of life in the city where it was born. You could easily base your entire stay around this sensual art form—the dance, its music and the world of tango.

Mysterious Origins

Few cities are as closely linked to a music-and-dance form as Buenos Aires is to tango, the origins of which are lost in the back alleys of the 19th-century port. It is hard to believe that this elegant dance emerged from such a sordid underworld, but in Buenos Aires even the down-at-heel have always been smart. The city that gave birth to tango was a hybrid place, where immigrants from Europe, Afro-Argentine slaves and gaucho cowboys, tempted by city life, intermingled. They forged an expression through slang lyrics based on Genoese dialect, rhythms from polka and Spanish folk dance and an attitude combining melancholy with knife-fighting swagger.

Rejection and Acceptance

The first records of tango appear in the 1870s, but by the early 20th century tango switched from a subversive outpouring for the working classes to an elevated art form admired by wealthier Porteños. The first tango in Paris (1913), to coin a phrase, was a seal of wider approval, confirmed by news that even British royalty danced it. Another leap forward was the recording of 'Mi Noche Triste' by Carlos Gardel (▷ 73) in 1917—his career took off in the 1920s when a sophisticated variant of tango reached dance halls across the city. In its heyday, a galaxy of stars, poet-lyricists and musicians won the people's hearts, but reactionary governments tried to ban tango. General Perón, though, ever the populist, declared it the national dance in the 1940s.

Clockwise from top: Tango dancing in the street in La Boca; the sign for El Balcon's tango-dinner show; a tango singer in San Telmo; the tango show at Esquina

The *Bandoneón*

No *orquesta típica* (traditional ensemble) is worth its salt without at least one *bandoneón*, a concertina that is placed on a blanket to stop all the movement wearing out the player's knee fabric. Invented in Germany as a peripatetic church-organ, the *bandoneón* was adopted by the tango ensembles because its mournful wheezing and offbeat timbre seemed to suit the tango mood perfectly. It usually appears alongside a piano, a couple of fiddles and a double bass.

New Tango

Successive innovations have since transformed tango—musician Astor Piazzolla helped to invent Nuevo Tango, a modern take with strong overtones of jazz, but from the 1960s on many Argentines increasingly looked on tango as old-fashioned. Part of its revival has been tourism-driven, after visitors voiced their amazement at the fact that tango was not more prominent in Porteño cultural life. New electronic sounds have given tango another shot in the arm and Buenos Aires has become the world's tango capital once more.

Stilettos and Sextets

Most visitors to the city make do with one of the many tango dinner-shows on offer—and some of them are truly spectacular, all fashion-model looks and mind-boggling flashings of stilettos between sharply creased trouser legs. You will also be treated to impromptu displays of street tango, as couples show off the steps and a third character passes round a fedora for a coin. Yet tango is as much about the entrancing music as fishnet stockings and cheek-to-cheek strutting. Do try and attend at least one tango music concert during your stay. The Sexteto Mayor, created in 1973, may not have all its founding members but it remains one of tango's leading bands.

Homero Manzi; tango shoes and tango-related items are sold in specialist shops; painting a tango scene

Top Tips For...

These great suggestions will help you tailor your ideal visit to Buenos Aires, no matter how you choose to spend your time.

...Keeping the Kids Happy
Visit the vintage ships moored in **Los Diques de Puerto Madero** (▷ 28–29).
Ogle at penguins and observe llamas in Palermo's **Jardín Zoológico** (▷ 70).
Have a fun day out at the **Parque de la Costa** theme park (▷ 63).

...Communing with Nature
Learn about the birds and the trees in the **Jardín Botánico** (▷ 32–33).
Picnic, along with everyone else, in the **Parque Tres de Febrero** (▷ 20–21).
Kayak in subtropical **El Tigre** (▷ 62–63).
Go on a guided walk around the **Reserva Ecológica Costanera Sur** (▷ 26–27).

...Retail Therapy
Visit the **Palermo Queen** (▷ 126, panel).
Kit out your kids at **Mimo & Co** (▷ 125).
Rummage through fans and figurines at **Gil Antigüedades** (▷ 124).
Mosey round the malls—try **Patio Bullrich** for size (▷ 126).

...Spectator Sports
Watch a chukka or two at the **Campo Argentino de Polo** (▷ 134).
Cheer on the home side (it's safer!) at **La Bombonera** (▷ 18–19).

...Art and Antiques
Hunt for a bargain in the **Feria de San Telmo** and around (▷ 53).
Discover **Xul Solar** (▷ 48–49).
Attend the **ArteBA show** (May/June ▷ 162).
Compare European and Argentine masters in **Museo Nacional de Bellas Artes** (▷ 46–47).

Clockwise from top: Patio Bullrich mall, bustling with shops, restaurants and cinemas; venerable Teatro

…Brunch
Savour smoked salmon washed down with vodka at **Ølsen** (▷ 148).
Go for the chic option at **Sirop Folie** (▷ 150).
Stay healthy with an organic brunch at **Orígen** in San Telmo (▷ 148).

…Live Music
Test the acoustics at the world-class **Teatro Colón** (▷ 60–61).
Hear top Latin American musicians at **ND/ Ateneo** (▷ 136).
Tap your feet at **Thelonious** jazz club (▷ 137).
Listen to the best in orchestral tango at the **Centro Cultural Torquato Tasso** (▷ 134).

…Lingering Over a Coffee
Accept you're a tourist at the famous **Café Tortoni** (▷ 144).
Soak up the retro ambience at **Florida Garden** (▷ 146).
Be cool and have a cappuccino at the **MALBA café** (▷ 30–39).
Taste blueberries at **b-Blue Deli and Natural Bar**—but you can have coffee, too (▷ 142).

…Discovering Evita
Find out who she was at the **Museo Evita** (▷ 40–41).
Make the pilgrimage to her grave at the **Cementerio de la Recoleta** (▷ 24–25).
See where she fired up the crowds: the balcony of the **Casa Rosada** (▷ 55).

…Browsing in Bookshops
Sip coffee and wonder at the world's most beautiful bookshop, the **Ateneo Grand Splendid** (▷ 121).
Ask for literary advice at the historic **Librería de Ávila** (▷ 70–71).
Thumb through old tomes at **Alberto Casares** (▷ 121).

Colón; a fine art gallery in Palermo; Tienda Diversia shop; trendy Ølsen restaurant

Timeline

1516 Portuguese explorer Juan Díaz de Solís lands at the site of Buenos Aires, but is killed by natives.

1536 The city of Buenos Aires is founded in present-day San Telmo on 2 February by a Spanish expedition led by Pedro de Mendoza.

1580 The second founding of the city is led by Juan de Garay—this time it is permanent but the city remains a colonial backwater for decades.

1767 The Jesuits are expelled from the Spanish colonies by royal decree. The city is made the capital of the Viceroyalty a year later.

1806 British troops invade but are beaten back ('Reconquista') by local forces led by Santiago de Liniers.

1807 The British make a second unsuccessful attempt to take over the city—their defeat is known as 'La Defensa'.

1810 The May Revolution (25 May) marks the first step towards independence of the United Provinces of the River Plate.

1853 Buenos Aires Province secedes from the rest of the United Provinces of the River Plate for seven years.

1871 A yellow fever epidemic results in a mass migration of the middle classes from San Telmo to Recoleta.

1880 The Federal Republic comes into being with Buenos Aires as the capital. The Casa Rosada becomes the presidential residence and Torcuato de Alvear is appointed city mayor.

1908 The Teatro Colón is inaugurated after construction work taking nearly 25 years.

1910 Centenary celebrations see countless monuments erected, most of them donated by the different ethnic communities.

Eva Perón lies in state in the General Confederation of Labour building in 1952

The facade of the famous Teatro Colón

1943 Military coup against civilian government. General Perón is active in new government.

1945 Under pressure from the military, Perón resigns and is arrested. The 17 October demonstration leads to his release and eventually to his first presidency.

1952 At Eva Perón's funeral, one of the country's biggest ever, eight mourners are crushed to death.

1978 Argentina hosts and wins the soccer World Cup against a background of state terror, the Dirty War.

1992 A huge bomb destroys the Israeli embassy, killing 29 people. Two years later another terrorist attack hits a Jewish association and claims 85 lives.

1993 Constitutional change allows mayoral elections—the first vote takes place in 1996 (Fernando de la Rúa becomes mayor).

Detail of a door, Teatro Colón

2001 A political crisis explodes in December, forcing President de la Rúa to leave Casa Rosada by helicopter. More than 20 people are killed during violent street demonstrations in the downtown.

2004 On 30 December a fire engulfs the Cromagnón nightclub, killing 200 and leading to tighter safety rules.

2007 Mauricio Macri, President of Boca Juniors Football Club, is elected mayor.

2010 The national bicentenary is celebrated with festivities, and the reopening of the Teatro Colón after extensive renovations.

THE CITY'S NAMES

When the Spanish founded the city in the 16th century they called it La Ciudad de la Santísima Trinidad y Puerto de Santa María de los Buenos Ayres (City of the Most Holy Trinity and Port of Saint Mary of the Fair Winds). That mouthful was shortened to Buenos Aires, or 'Baires', or even 'Biei' from the Anglo-Saxon pet name based on the city's initials. The city's natives are still called Porteños, from 'Puerto' while over the years Buenos Aires' many nicknames have included the Paris of the South, the Queen of the River Plate—and even the Great Udder, owing to its distinctive shape on the map.

MOTHERS OF THE PLAZA DE MAYO

From 1977 to 2006 the Madres (Mothers) and Abuelas (Grandmothers) of the Plaza de Mayo regularly marched around the plaza, wearing white headscarves to draw attention to the thousands of people who disappeared during the Dirty War (1976–83). They still gather there every Thursday to publicize social causes, but they called off their main demonstration in recognition of improved human rights across the country.

Top 25

This section contains the must-see Top 25 sights and experiences in Buenos Aires. They are listed alphabetically, and numbered so you can locate them on the inside front cover map.

HIGHLIGHTS

- Teatro Colón
- French Embassy
- Trees
- El Obelisco

TIPS

- Use the pedestrian crossings—and don't try to get to the other side in one go.
- Officially and confusingly the avenue has four names: Cerrito, Carlos Pellegrini, Bernardo de Yrigoyen and Lima.

The Avenida 9 de Julio defines Buenos Aires as clearly as it slices through it—big, bold and very difficult to get across. Its great icon, El Obelisco, also symbolizes the city's thrusting ambitions.

Vast *avenida* Named for Argentina's Independence Day, 9 July 1816, the city's most macho thoroughfare is a vociferous statement of urban planning, with its dozen traffic lanes and 6km (4 miles) of tarmac. Luckily, the concrete is alleviated by landscaped verges planted with jacarandas and other trees, where the song of the native *kiskadee* (a chirpy yellow bird) is just audible above the car horns. Opened in 1937, it was created by tearing down dozens of buildings but a few were spared, including the majestic French Embassy at the corner with

Clockwise from far left: Club Espanolo; people crossing the avenue; the view across the avenue to El Obelisco; a newsstand; Teatro Colón; a mural of the avenue's busy traffic

Avenida Alvear. However, the most imposing edifice on this central avenue has to be the Teatro Colón (▷ 60–61), the opera house.

Obvious obelisk If Buenos Aires has one symbolic monument it is the ivory-hued El Obelisco, a 67m (220ft) monolith marking the crossroads of Avenida 9 de Julio and Avenida Corrientes. Inaugurated in 1936 to celebrate the city's foundation in 1536, it hasn't always met with universal approval—there were even plans to demolish it in the 1940s. However, over the years the road encircling it has become a favourite venue for open-air concerts and victorious football fans, anti-government demos and, in bicentenary year (2010), major festivities. Featured on just about every postcard, it is a useful landmark for getting your bearings.

THE BASICS

➕ G6
🍴 Cafés and food stalls
🚇 Carlos Pellegrini (B), Diagonal Norte (C), 9 de Julio (D)
🚌 6, 7, 9, 10, 17, 23, 24, 26, 29, 45, 50, 70, 99, 109, 111, 142, 146, 155
♿ Adequate

HIGHLIGHTS

- Plaza de Mayo
- La Prensa
- Café Tortoni
- Edificio Barolo
- Palacio del Congreso

TIPS

- Keep away during political demonstrations as things can turn nasty.
- Quaint Subte Línea A runs beneath the avenue—Perú station is best.

This golden area, between parliament and the presidential headquarters, is lined by some fantastical buildings, including a skyscraper folly, inspired by Dante's *Divine Comedy*, and a former newspaper office.

Architectural showcase Most cities possess at least one iconic thoroughfare and Buenos Aires' is the Avenida de Mayo, built when the city underwent revolutionary urban planning in the 1880s. Only a dozen blocks long but amply wide and shaded by centennial trees, it is a showcase of beautiful buildings capped with curvaceous cupolas and Parisian-style mansards, while their elegant facades bristle with art nouveau and art deco detailing. Two of the city's greatest buildings stand at either end: Casa Rosada (▷ 55) and the Palacio del Congreso

Clockwise from far top left: The view over Plaza del Congreso from Edifico Barolo; the Inmobiliaria building is on the avenue; neo-baroque magnificence inside La Prensa; detail of the original elevator at Edifico Barolo; strolling along the avenue

(▷ 74). In between are more stupendous constructions, including the neo-baroque La Prensa, crowned with a bronze statue of Athena, and the fantastical Edificio Barolo (▷ 68).

Historic cafés Visitors flock to Café Tortoni, the city's most illustrious coffee house, to admire the sumptuous decor over an espresso. For much of the 20th century it was frequented by all the big tango personalities along with tittle-tattling politicians and revered intellectuals. It is still worth a visit, as long as you realize it is now a tourist trap. There are other history-steeped cafés to seek out, not least London City, at the corner with Calle Perú, where leading Argentine writer Julio Cortázar set his novel, *The Winners,* and the musty 36 Billares at No. 1265, where pool was first played in Argentina in 1882.

THE BASICS

🚋 G7
🍴 Cafés, bars and restaurants
🚇 Plaza de Mayo, Perú, Piedras, Avenida de Mayo, Lima, Sáenz Peña, Congreso
🚌 39, 60, 64, 168
♿ Adequate

3 La Bombonera—Boca Juniors Stadium

HIGHLIGHTS

- The stadium
- Soccer match
- Rock concert
- Museum

TIPS

- Attend a match through an organized trip—by the club itself (see the website) or a tourist agency.
- Do not linger around the stadium at night and do not wander off the beaten track even in the daytime.

In their day, Diego Maradona and Carlos Tévez both wowed Boca Junior fans on the turf. If you can't make it to a match, try a guided tour.

The Chocolate Box Built in 1940 and renovated in the 1990s, the Estadio Alberto J. Armando is Boca Juniors' home ground. It is fondly known as La Bombonera ('Chocolate Box') because of its size—the capacity is a mere 49,000—and unusual steep-sided shape, like an old-fashioned box of soft centres. Attending a match here is an unforgettable experience— the raucous Boca fans are known as the team's 12th man and their motto is 'La Bombonera does not tremble, it beats like a heart'. The Superclásico derby where they play against their fierce rivals, River Plate, is deemed to be one of

Clockwise from far left: La Bombonera stadium; a mural of Diego Maradona, who played for Boca Juniors; a sea of blue and yellow at a Juniors match in the stadium; the stadium's museum; a soccer match in progress

the most exciting matches in the soccer world. Such is the deep-seated rivalry that the Coca-Cola billboards in the stadium are uniquely black and white to avoid using River Plate's red-and-white strip.

Passion for the game For a stadium tour, visit the two-floor Museo de la Pasión Boquense. Exhibits include a large mural of Maradona and a giant 'football' screening 360-degree footage of players and fans at a match. One interesting fact, illustrated in an oil painting here, is that Boca originally played in different colours but in 1906 decided to look for a new strip, which would be based on the flag of the first ship to sail into the port. As that ship was the Swedish *Drottning Sophia*, blue and yellow were the adopted colours.

THE BASICS

www.museoboquense.com

♦ J11

✉ Brandsen 805, Boca

☎ 4362-1100

🕐 Daily 10–6 (may differ on home match days)

🍴 Refreshment outlets

🚌 25, 46, 86, 152

♿ Few

💰 Moderate

HIGHLIGHTS

● The boating lake
● The Rosedal
● The Patio Andaluz
● The Jardín de los Poetas
● Museo Sívori
● Jardín Japonés

TIPS

● On summer weekends, the parks get crowded but you should be able to find some space of your own.
● Avoid the parks after dusk and, during the day, do not wander off the main paths if you are alone.

A verdant chunk of Palermo is given over to parks and gardens, known collectively as the Bosques ('Woodlands'). The centrepiece Parque Tres de Febrero, takes its name from a famous battle in which a 19th-century despot was defeated.

Green, green grass Some 5sq km (2sq miles) of northern Palermo, the Bosques de Palermo, are taken up by parkland as well as the national racecourse (Hipódromo Argentino ▷ 70), the major polo fields (▷ 134) and a colourful rose garden. Ducks and geese swim in three great artificial lakes where you can row a boat, while the large park is a popular setting for biking and in-line skating, jogging or just kicking a football around. The lawns and sweeping paths are often thronged with people enjoying

Clockwise from far left: Blue skies and palms are a big attraction in Palermo's park; El Rosedal—the rose garden; Planetario Galileo Galilei; the Jardín Japonés is a popular attraction; hockey is just one of the sports that are played in the park

their leisure time, while extended families enjoy picnics by the lakes.

Added attractions At the eastern edge of these playing grounds, in the Parque Tres de Febrero, stands the Planetario Galileo Galilei (▷ 76), a fun place for astronomy fans. Nearby a boating lake beckons, as does one of the city's best collections of Argentine art, in the Museo Sívori (▷ 73). To the west, by the rose garden, an Andalucian patio rewards exploration as does the Jardín de los Poetas, where internationally renowned bards are commemorated with bronze and marble busts. This set of gardens is completed by the Jardín Japonés, graced by bonsais and gingkos, azaleas and flowering almonds and set off by red bridges and ponds inhabited by shoals of coy carp.

THE BASICS

www.bue.gov.ar
www.jardinjapones.org.ar

➕ B2

✉ Jardín Japonés:
Avenida Casares and Berro

☎ Jardín Japonés: 4804-4922

🕐 Jardín Japonés: daily 10–6

🍴 Cafés and food stalls

🚇 Scalabrini Ortiz

🚌 34, 67, 130

♿ Satisfactory

💵 Parque: free; Jardín Japonés: inexpensive

5 El Caminito

HIGHLIGHTS

● Arts and crafts fair
● Tango displays
● The vibrant colours of the houses

TIPS

● Do not stray too far away from the Caminito itself: This is a very poor district and any valuables will attract unwanted attention.
● Enjoy the view of the two fabulous bridges over the Riachuelo: the Puente Transbordador and the Puente Nicolás Avellaneda.

Boca's most famous street isn't a street at all, but a colourful example of urban recycling. A disused railway siding was turned into one of the city's best-known tourist sights thanks to a brainwave by local painter, Quinquela Martín.

Recuperation Colourful open-air museum El Caminito (The Little Way) was a derelict railway siding until the 1950s, when local artist Benito Quinquela Martín (1890–1977) transformed it into an alfresco tableau. He had the brilliant idea of using leftover boat paint to brighten up the rickety corrugated-iron shacks lining the street, a Genoese custom. The result was a striking backdrop of soothing pastel tones clashing with more vibrant shades of yellow, blue and red—a riot of colour that finds its way

Clockwise from left: Brightly painted, narrow buildings in El Caminito; tango displays in the street, known as 'tango alley', are a feature of the district

on to many a postcard and calendar. Note that Boca is regarded as one of the least salubrious neighbourhoods, so you should not stray too far: Some of the toughest tenement blocks in the city lurk menacingly close by.

Tango alley The name comes from a 1920s tango song 'Caminito' by Juan de Dios Filiberto and Gabino Coria Peñaloza—its mournful lyrics include the lines 'Little road covered in thistles/ The hand of time your track has erased/I'd like to fall by your wayside/And for time to kill us both'. These days it acts as a stage for showy tango, with pairs of dancers regularly displaying their talent to the wonderment of onlookers. There is also a daytime arts and crafts fair all along the Caminito where you can find some real gems among the tacky souvenirs.

THE BASICS

✚ J12
✉ El Caminito, Boca
🍴 Cafés, bars and restaurants
🚌 29, 53, 64, 152
♿ Adequate

HIGHLIGHTS

- The site
- Evita's tomb
- The mausoleums
- The Alvear family vault
- William Brown's grave

TIPS

- It is a good idea to consult the best website about the graves at www.urbex.com.ar.
- There are guided tours in Spanish Mar–Nov, every last Sun at 2.30pm and English Tue, Thu at 11am.

The great and good of Argentina are buried in Recoleta's eye-catching cemetery, though most visitors are only interested in one tomb, that of Eva Perón, whose corpse had to be smuggled in at night.

Grandiose graves Perhaps the most exclusive and photogenic graveyard on Earth, La Recoleta began life as a humble burial ground in 1822. As the *barrio* became the place to live in the 1870s, its denizens needed a suitable cemetery to honour their deceased and it came to resemble a whimsical town within the city—so eerily sculpted and chiselled it resembles an Escher drawing. It has been called a tribute to the great civilizations of the past, from Babylonian to Byzantine, and Egyptian to Italian Renaissance. Its great mausoleums hewn from

Clockwise from far left: Many tombs in the cemetery are adorned with statues; Eva Perón's tomb is the most visited in the cemetery, but is one of the plainest; views across the tombs; some of the many family mausoleums; buildings huddle around the cemetery

granite and marble are decorated with bronze and gold, and adorned with delicate angels and solemn busts. Like the feral cats here, just prowl among the melancholy splendour.

Who's who? Most visitors make straight for the plain Duarte family vault where Eva Perón was laid to rest in the 1970s; although the cemetery authorities disapproved of having the anti-establishment First Lady interred among the country's wealthiest and most aristocratic citizens. It is well worth spending more time to wander for a look at more ornate tombs. Not far from the monumental entrance is the majestic tomb of the influential Alvear family. Seek out the central plaza for the original resting place of Irish admiral William Brown, decorated with a miniature frigate.

THE BASICS

www.cementeriorecoleta.com.ar

➕ E4

✉ Avenida Quintana and Junín 1760, Recoleta

☎ 4803-1594

🕐 Daily 7–5.45

🍴 La Biela (▷ 143)

🚌 10, 17, 60, 67, 92, 110

♿ Adequate

✋ Free

HIGHLIGHTS

- The pampas grass
- Picnicking
- Birdlife
- Moonlight walks

TIPS

- There are frequent guided walks with explanations of the flora and fauna. They take place on weekends at 10.30 and 3.30, plus night tours during full moon.
- Take plenty of water, use sunscreen and wear a sunhat during the day, and in the evening apply insect repellent liberally.

The riverside half of swish Puerto Madero is an ecological reserve: Huge lagoons host flocks of water birds while the surrounding greenery is favoured by bikers and joggers, birders and lizards.

Environmentally friendly The sandy polders and shallow lagoons on the riverside of Puerto Madero's docks and skyscrapers are protected as the Reserva Ecológica Costanera Sur. More than 2km (1.6 miles) in length and covering a total of 350ha (865 acres), the reserve is a mass of dense grasses and nodding reeds, including the famed pampas grass, whose golden plumes frame every view. This wonderful green lung delights city-dwellers and visitors alike: In addition to avid joggers and casual ramblers, the Costanera attracts myriad birds,

Clockwise from left: The view across the Costanera to city skyscrapers; couples strolling along the Costanera Sur; families enjoy bicycle trips here; an aerobics class; pampas grass grows everywhere in the reserve

flamingos and parrots, great egrets and black-necked swans, which thrive in this astonishingly rural habitat of willows and acacias. Coypus, a kind of water rat, and lizards also love it here.

Nature lovers Your first port of call should be the visitor centre, just inside the main entrance. There you will find friendly staff, who can fix up guided tours of the reserve. You can also study the useful display panels, which explain in detail the flora and fauna that you are likely to see during your tour. The easiest and shortest trail around the Laguna de los Patos will take you about two relaxed hours. There are benches for taking a rest, a picnic area (first stock up at I Fresh Market, ▷ 147 or I Central Market, ▷ 124) and even a small beach on the banks of the Río de la Plata.

THE BASICS

🔢 J6

✉️ Puerto Madero

☎️ 4893-1640 or 0800 444 5343 (freephone)

🕐 Apr–Oct Tue–Sun 8–6; Nov–Mar 8–7

🍴 Cafés and restaurants in Puerto Madero

🚇 Leandro N. Alem

🚌 26, 61, 93, 152, 159, 195

♿ Adequate

🆓 Free

HIGHLIGHTS

● The docks and ships
● Fragata *Presidente Sarmiento*
● Corbeta *Uruguay*
● Puente de la Mujer
● Colección de Arte Amalia Lacroze de Fortabat

TIPS

● The bridge at the northern end of the *diques* is often opened for maritime traffic—you might find yourself cut off for a while from terra firma.
● Do not underestimate the distances—the docklands are huge.

Two historic naval vessels, a futuristic bridge and a world-class art collection all lurk in the Puerto Madero docklands, where restored brick warehouses function as top-flight hotels and classy restaurants.

Historic ships Four rectangular *diques* (docks), numbered 1 to 4 from south to north, form a watery chain along the eastern limit of downtown, where some of the city's most expensive real estate is to be found in converted Madero warehouses. Dique 3 is crossed by a streamlined white footbridge by internationally acclaimed Spanish architect Santiago Calatrava, El Puente de la Mujer (Woman's Bridge), a physical reminder that all thoroughfares in the *barrio* are unusually named after female personalities. Two

Clockwise from left: ARA Presidente Sarmiento is one of the major attractions in the docks; Cabañas Las Lilas restaurant is at Dique 3; Puerto Madero bridge; a nighttime view over Puerto Madero; former warehouses along the dock are now mostly occupied by restaurants and cafés

---

THE BASICS

✚ J8
✉ Puerto Madero.
Colección de Arte Amalia
Lacroze de Fortabat: Olga
Cossettini 141
☎ Fragata *Presidente
Sarmiento:* 4334-9336;
Colección Fortabat: 4310-
6600
🕐 Fragata ARA *Presidente
Sarmiento:* daily 9–8;
Corbeta *Uruguay:* daily
10–9; Colección Fortabat:
Tue–Sun 12–9. Guided
visits 3 and 5pm
🍴 Cafés, bars and
restaurants
🚇 Leandro N. Alem
🚌 26, 61, 93, 152, 159,
195; Colección Fortabat: 2,
6, 20, 61, 130, 140. Tranvia
del Este (Puerto Madero
Tramway; ▷ 167)
♿ Adequate
🎫 Fragata *Presidente
Sarmiento* and Corbeta
Uruguay: inexpensive;
Colección Fortabat:
moderate

---

beautifully preserved British-built, 19th-century sailing ships, the frigate ARA *Presidente Sarmiento* and the corvette ARA *Uruguay,* are usually moored at Diques 3 and 4, respectively, and are worth a visit to see their interiors.

World-class art At the top of Dique 4, a purpose-built edifice with a curved roof houses one of the country's finest private art collections on public display: The Colección de Arte Amalia Lacroze de Fortabat. Named after one of the richest women in the country, this museum, in addition to outstanding works by Argentine artists and Egyptian artefacts, includes paintings by J.M.W. Turner, Pieter Brueghel the Younger and Jan Brueghel, plus paintings and sculptures by Salvador Dali, Marc Chagall and Auguste Rodin, among other great names.

Shopping is the Porteños' third religion after football and tango. This vaulted shrine to consumerism is where many come to worship, taking time off to enjoy an ice cream, drink a coffee or watch a film.

Mall art Buenos Aires has the most elegant shopping malls in the world but downtown Galerías Pacífico turns consumerism into an art form. Housed in a stunning 1889 beaux-arts building, it was originally a branch of Parisian department store Au Bon Marché. Over the elegant central atrium you will see a dozen bright frescoes executed in 1946 by leading Argentine artists, including Lino Enea Spilimbergo, Antonio Berni and Demetrio Urruchúa. When the building was renovated in the 1990s after years of neglect, another four

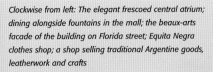

Clockwise from left: The elegant frescoed central atrium; dining alongside fountains in the mall; the beaux-arts facade of the building on Florida street; Equita Negra clothes shop; a shop selling traditional Argentine goods, leatherwork and crafts

frescoes were added for good measure. The upper floor is partly occupied by the Centro Cultural Borges (▷ 134)—where you can dip into temporary exhibitions or learn to tango.

Down to business The Galerías may appear like an art gallery, but there's some serious purse-emptying to be done. You might like to buy a new one at a branch of Casa López, while a huge range of local and international clothing brands have stores here. Cúspide is one of the best bookshop chains in the country and its ground-floor store is a great place to pick up a coffee-table book. If gazing at frescoes and shopping for gifts proves too much, you can sample succulent pasta at Francesca or indulge in a *dulce de leche* ice cream at Freddo, down in the airy food patio.

THE BASICS

www.progaleriaspacifico.
com.ar
➕ G6
✉ Florida and Avenida Córdoba, City Centre
☎ 5555-5110
🕐 Mon–Sat 10–9, Sun 12–9
🍴 Food patio in basement
🚇 Florida/San Martín
🚌 6, 33, 45, 50, 61, 109, 115, 130, 140, 152, 195
♿ Satisfactory

HIGHLIGHTS

● La Casona
● The glasshouses
● Sculptures

TIP

● There are regular guided visits, weather permitting: Sat, Sun and national holidays 10.30, 3.30 and 4.30. In the summer there are also evening tours at 9pm.

Designed by and named after French botanist, Charles 'Carlos' Thays, this tranquil triangle at the heart of Palermo is home to more than 5,000 trees and shrubs, including *ceibos* and *tipas*, oaks and *ombúes*.

Prolific Frenchman The botanical garden, inaugurated in the 1890s, was for many years home to the great landscape artist Thays (1849–1934), while he was director of the city parks. He and his family occupied the English-style brick mansion—La Casona—that now houses the administration and information centre. One of the five magnificent glasshouses near by is a huge wrought-iron construction that won high acclaim at the 1889 Paris Universal Exhibition. It now shelters more than 2,000 tropical plants, many of them native to

TOP 25

Left: Statues are a feature of the gardens—this is at the entrance near Carlos Thays' former home; below: A statue of Mercury stands near one of the gardens' magnificent glasshouses

Argentina. The 7ha (17-acre) garden also hosts a sizeable population of abandoned cats, tended by a dedicated group of volunteers. Most of the grounds are laid out by geographical theme, with areas for each region of Argentina, making it a great place to learn about native flora.

Sculptures Another highlight of the Jardín Botánico is its collection of sculptures, busts and other monuments. These include a small bronze of Thays himself near the Casona, and a statue of Mercury overlooking the Roman garden, a grove of cypresses and laurels. The centrepiece of the Italianate garden near the entrance is an unmissable circular lily pond adorned with an enchanting statue of a nymph, *Ondina del Plata*, by Lía Correa Morales.

THE BASICS

www.buenosaires.gov.ar
+ B3
✉ Plaza Italia, Palermo
☎ 4831-4527
🕐 Summer 8–7; winter 8–6
🚇 Plaza Italia
🚌 39, 59, 60 152
♿ Satisfactory
🆓 Free

HIGHLIGHTS

- Interiors
- Tunnels
- Aula Magna
- Iglesia San Ignacio

TIPS

- The guided tours are excellent and it is worth planning ahead for the English version.
- Check the website or local listings for news of concerts and other events.

The city's oldest church and Argentina's most prestigious secondary school share this solid block of colonial buildings, offering an opportunity to find out more about the intriguing history of Buenos Aires.

Intellectual block The Jesuits promoted intellectual pursuits and played a vital role in Argentine history, as testified by the Manzana de las Luces (Block of Enlightenment). Occupying a complete block, of which some original buildings remain, it was the Society of Jesus' national headquarters from the 1670s until the 1760s, but its present name was not coined until the early 19th century. To this day the *manzana* comprises a collection of prized educational institutions, including the Colegio Nacional (CNBA), a high school. Its present

Clockwise from left: Iglesia San Ignacio; tours visit the 18th-century tunnels under the complex; an imposing corridor in the Colegio Nacional high school; the Sala de Representantes hosts concerts and events

home was built in the early 20th century, in an austere but imposing French Academic style.

Inside view Try to join a tour for a glimpse of the atmospheric patios and chambers plus the 18th-century tunnels once used for smuggling. The highlight, the CNBA's majestic Aula Magna—where graduation ceremonies are held—was inspired by Opéra Garnier in Paris. At the corner of Calles Alsina and Bolívar, San Ignacio is the city's oldest church still standing, built by the Jesuits in 1675. The baroque altar and 17th-century icon of Nuestra Señora de las Nieves date from the church's construction. Concerts and other events regularly enliven the courtyards and the Sala de Representantes, a semicircular chamber where Buenos Aires' first provincial parliament met in the 19th century.

THE BASICS

www.manzanadelasluces.gov.ar

⊕ G8

✉ Perú 272, City Centre

☎ 4342-3964

🕐 For guided visits see website. Visits in English must be booked two weeks in advance.

🚇 Perú, Plaza de Mayo

🚌 2, 23, 91, 98

♿ Inexpensive

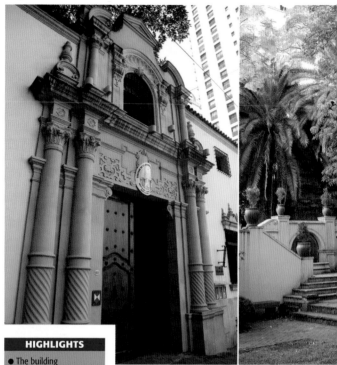

HIGHLIGHTS

- The building
- The tabernacle
- Guaraní statues
- Paintings from Cusco
- The garden

TIPS

- Don't miss the basement, for interesting exhibits of silverware, clothing and a reconstructed colonial kitchen.
- The garden is wonderfully relaxing.
- Find out about the classical concerts held inside the house—these are usually advertised at the entrance.

This museum is one of the city's finest tributes to its Hispanic past, sometimes forgotten among all its Parisian palaces and Italianate mansions. The exquisite exterior of the neo-baroque house is matched by the first-rate Spanish-American art inside.

Neocolonial revival The museum of Spanish-American art is named after a wealthy engineer and prolific art collector. On his death in 1928 the collection was bequeathed to the city, which housed it in the Palacio Noel. The style of this Retiro palace, built in the 1920s by architect Martín Noel, who donated it to the city in 1936, was inspired by the baroque buildings of 18th-century Lima and the white walls, intricate window-grilles and Peruvian balconies make it the ideal home for the artefacts inside.

Clockwise from left: Palacio Noel is dwarfed by skyscrapers; the museum's gardens are an attraction in their own right; the magnificent setting for the treasures in the collection; Palacio Noel was donated to the city by its architect, Martín Noel

The colonial collection Most of the works were produced in colonial Peru and Alto Peru (Bolivia): The ground-floor highlight is an ornate 18th-century silver tabernacle adorned with a portrait of Christ. Look, too, for polychrome furniture made by Bolivian craftspeople and, on the walls, a fine set of Guaraní statues, carved from native wood at the Jesuit missions. Upstairs a series of rooms filled with paintings and furniture illustrates the growing confidence of Buenos Aires as it became a serious rival to Lima following the creation of the Viceroyalty of the River Plate in 1776. One interesting installation illustrates the importance of the silversmiths of Potosí, while in another you see how porcelain and tortoiseshell items from the Philippines became fashionable in the lead-up to Argentine independence.

THE BASICS

www.museofernandez
blanco.buenosaires.gob.ar

➕ G5

✉ Suipacha 1422, Retiro

☎ 4327-0228

🕐 Tue–Fri and national hols 2–7, Sat–Sun 12–7

🍴 Cafés and restaurants nearby in Retiro

🚌 93, 130, 152

♿ Few

💲 Inexpensive

13 Museo de Arte Latinoamericano de Buenos Aires (MALBA)

HIGHLIGHTS

● The contemporary architecture
● The bookshop and café
● Works by Frida Kahlo and Guillermo Kuitca

TIPS

● On Wednesday the museum closes later and the admission price is lower.
● Visit the shop (Tiendamalba) and check out the cinema (malba.cine).
● Guided tours on Wednesday and Sunday at 4pm are in Spanish but you can call ahead for an English-speaking guide.

One of the most important collections of modern Latin American art anywhere, the MALBA (Museum of Latin American Art of Buenos Aires) is an exciting museum, superbly packaged in a modern building.

World-class architecture Ensconced in its showpiece Palermo building, this stunning museum has attracted eager crowds to its refined permanent collection and excellent temporary exhibitions ever since it opened in 2001. Three architects from Córdoba, Gastón Atelman, Martín Fourcade and Alfredo Tapia, won the competition to build its home. Their edifice is regarded as one of the best modern buildings in the city. Clean lines, huge plate-glass windows and efficient use of space are some of its plus points.

Clockwise from left: Café des Arts is the on-site restaurant; art is displayed on various levels; the museum shop sells all manner of enticing items; the exterior of the modern showpiece building; *Los Viudos* by Fernando Botero

Latin American masterpieces The MALBA's core is the Costantini Collection, representing nearly 80 artists. Every modern artistic movement and just about every Latin American country are represented in the permanent collection. From the 1930s, Joaquín Torres-García's monochrome *Composition symétrique universelle en blanc et noir* contrasts with Emilio Di Cavalcanti's colourful *Mulheres com frutas*. Leading 1940s' artists, Mexican Frida Kahlo (*Autorretrato con chango y loro*) and Cuban Wilfredo Lam (*La mañana verde*), both have a painting on display. Works by contemporary creators, like Argentine Guillermo Kuitca (*Siete últimas canciones*), bring the collection up to date. Temporary shows have been dedicated to individual artists, including non-Latin Americans like Andy Warhol and Roy Lichtenstein.

THE BASICS

www.malba.org.ar

⊞ D3

✉ Avenida Figueroa Alcorta 3415, Palermo

☎ 4808-6511

🕐 Mon, Thu–Sun 12–8, Wed 12–9

🍴 Café des Arts (tel: 4808 0754, open daily 9am–midnight)

🚌 67, 102, 130

♿ Good

💰 Moderate; Wed inexpensive

- The building
- Footage of the 'Don't Cry for Me' speech
- The Luis Agostino dress worn during the triumphant European tour

TIP

- The temporary exhibitions about Evita and related subjects are often very good.

Evita must be the most famous Argentine woman in history—yet all most people know about her comes from the musical or movie. You can find out more at this fascinating Palermo museum.

Suitable setting It was five decades after her death before a museum dedicated to Argentina's most famous First Lady, Eva Duarte Perón (1919–52), was finally created. Appropriately it is in a remodelled town house that was home to Evita's Social Aid Foundation from 1948 until her death from cervical cancer. The attractive two-floor building is housed in a typical neocolonial mansion with a neo-Renaissance facade. It hosts a well-thought-out exhibition that traces Evita's short but dramatic life.

Left: The museum is in a former town house from which one of Eva Perón's foundations operated; below: A section of the museum devoted to Evita's final year

ETERNA
EVITA
1951-1952
Su último año

Rags to adulation Eva Duarte was born into a modest family in Buenos Aires Province and she came to the city to make it big as an actress. Juan Perón spotted her at a charity event in Luna Park (▷ 71) and they were soon married—and she was forced to give up her acting career. She played a leading role in Perón's election to the presidency, made a much publicized tour of Europe, and was even due to run as vice president but backed down, making the speech that inspired the song 'Don't Cry for Me, Argentina' in the musical and film. Historic footage of Evita's early films and passionate political rallies, plus photos and clothes from the chic wardrobe with which she wooed European leaders and audiences, tell Evita's story in intriguing detail. Recordings of Gotan Project's electric tango add to the ambience.

THE BASICS

www.museoevita.org

➕ B3

✉ Lafinur 2988, Palermo

☎ 4807-9433

🕐 May–Oct Tue–Sun 1–7; Nov–Apr 11–7. Also open holiday Mon

🍴 Ground-floor café

🚇 Plaza Italia/Scalabrini Ortiz

🚌 37, 59

♿ Few

💲 Moderate

HIGHLIGHTS

- The building
- Portrait of Rivadavia
- Oil of Beresford's defeat
- Tarja de Potosí

TIP

- Don't miss the fascinating section on the Afro-Argentine community that was key to Porteño life around the time of Independence—President Rivadavia was part African.

Columbus, Magellan and all the big names from Argentine history look down from their noble portraits in the national history museum, housed in a beautiful neocolonial mansion.

Historic house Argentina's major history museum is housed in an Italianate mansion. The house belonged to José Gregorio Lezama, who gave his name to the San Telmo park where it is located. The striking mid-19th-century burgundy and cream building housed the national historical museum after Lezama's death, when the park became state property. Extensive restoration in the early 21st century improved the presentation of the exhibits, which are chiefly of interest to fans of 19th-century political and military history.

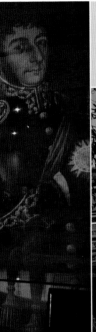

Left: Find out about the history of Argentina at the National History Museum; below: The museum is housed in an attractive neocolonial building

Hall of fame The exhibition inside the museum takes you on a chronological tour of Argentine history, with emphasis on majestic portraits of the leading lights. One that stands out is the depiction of Bernardino Rivadavia, the first president of independent Argentina. Another interesting canvas brings to life General Beresford, the British invader who was humiliatingly defeated by locals at the beginning of the 19th century—his shame was made worse by the lowly nature of the defending forces, as can be seen in the painting. The highlight of the collection is the magnificent gold-and-silver shield, the Tarja de Potosí. A masterpiece of fine craftwork, it was given to Argentine hero General Belgrano by the womenfolk of Potosí (Bolivia), out of gratitude for his role in freeing their country from colonial Spanish rule.

THE BASICS

- H10
- Defensa 1600, San Telmo
- 4307-1182
- Tue–Sun 11–6
- Caseros (▷ 145)
- 10, 24, 29, 39, 64, 130, 152
- Few
- Inexpensive

16 Museo Nacional de Arte Decorativo

When a Chilean diplomat and his wife needed a French mansion in Buenos Aires, René Sergent obliged with the Palacio Errázuriz, partly inspired by Versailles and now the national museum of decorative art.

Happy marriage Chilean Matías Errázuriz married Josefina Alvear, a daughter of the extremely wealthy Argentinian family, in Buenos Aires cathedral in 1897. They spent their early married years in Paris, amassing a magnificent collection of European furniture and artworks. Back in Buenos Aires in 1916, they required a house big enough and stylish enough to show off their spoils; French architect René Sergent (1865–1927), who designed many patrician homes in the Argentine capital, created a fabulous mansion, built using only European

Clockwise from left: The mansion that houses the museum was completed in 1918; the Gothic chapel; the boudoir was painted by José Sert; chandeliers light the chapel

materials and inaugurated in 1918 with a ball. Arthur Rubinstein once performed in the Grand Hall, and Anna Pavlova danced there—in fact the house saw some of the most exclusive events ever held in the city.

Decorous arts Later the family fell on hard times and sold their mansion to the state, which turned it into the Museo Nacional de Arte Decorativo (MNAD). The occasional concert and an annual carol service are held here, but the main reason for a visit is to see the superb collection of European cabinets and oils, silverware and tapestries. El Greco and Fragonard are just two of the artists represented here. Don't miss the boudoir painted by José María Sert, who decorated New York's Rockefeller Center.

THE BASICS

www.mnad.org.ar

➕ D3

✉ Avenida del Libertador 1902, Palermo

☎ 4801-8248

🕐 Tue–Sun 2–7; Jan–Feb closed Sun. Guided visits in English Tue, Wed–Sun 2.30

🍴 Croque Madame tearoom

🚌 10, 59, 60, 67, 130

♿ Few

💲 Inexpensive (Tue free); guided visits: inexpensive

HIGHLIGHTS

- Works by Rodin and Modigliani
- Hirsch Bequest
- Pre-Columbian collection and Mexican panels
- Room 107—Modern Argentine collection

TIPS

- You might like to make more than one visit as doing both floors in one go is quite a challenge.
- On the second floor there are interesting photographs and modern sculptures.
- Forget the recorded audio guide; the museum catalogue is a far better investment.

The MNBA (National Fine Arts Museum), in Recoleta, has such a vast collection of national and international artworks it can only show a fraction at a time. Even those paintings and sculptures will keep you busy for an hour or two.

Ground Floor, Old World Buenos Aires markets itself as a European city in the Americas, a claim shored up by this art collection. The museum building is a nondescript brick-red neoclassical pile but inside there are some sumptuous paintings and sculptures. One highlight is Room 3, housing the Hirsch Bequest, which features a Rembrandt portrait. The following rooms take you through 16th- and 17th-century European masters, with works by the likes of El Greco, Goya and Klee. Rodin

Clockwise from left: The facade is hung with posters for exhibitions; Naturaliza work by Lucio Fontana; La Terraza by Pablo Suárez; La Hamaca by Raúl Soldi; a gallery in the museum; Port of Buenos Aires by Richard Adams Smith

sculptures loom large as do some very fine pieces by Picasso, Modigliani and Kandinsky.

Upstairs, New World The first two rooms upstairs are cornucopias of pre-Columbian ceramics and textiles plus an unusual set of richly decorated panels from 18th-century Mexico. Early art depicting Argentina was mostly executed by foreigners but home-grown artists, such as Prilidiano Pueyrredón, started to shine through in the middle of the 19th century. By the early 20th century confidence matched the country's place in the world, evidenced by artists of the calibre of Sívori, Quinquela Martín and Fader. The 16-section Room 107 tours the modern period, dominated by Xul Solar, Pablo Suárez and Nicolás García Uriburu, each with very different styles.

THE BASICS

www.mnba.org.ar

🚌 E4

✉ Avenida del Libertador 1473, Recoleta

☎ 5288-9900

🕐 Tue–Fri 12.30–8.30, Sat–Sun, hols 9.30–8.30

🍴 Café

🚌 17, 62, 67, 93, 130

♿ Good

🆓 Free

HIGHLIGHTS

- The building
- *Entierro* (1915)
- *Casas en Alto* (1922)
- *Plurentes* (1949)
- *Pan Altar Mundi* (1954)
- *Hía tiu pre ver* (1962)

TIP

● Keep a look out for the work of the month—the museum selects one work and offers a detailed description of its depiction and conception.

If you want to focus on one Argentine artist, try the thought-provoking Museo Xul Solar. Solar's intricate watercolours and playful temperas reflect his offbeat worldview.

Leading light The only Argentine artist to have a museum in the capital dedicated exclusively to his work, Oscar Agustín Alejandro Schulz Solari (1887–1963), better known as Xul Solar, took his pseudonym not only from his real surnames but also as a mystical reference to the solar system and the Latin word *lux* (light), spelled backwards. A fascinating polymath, Solar produced myriad distinctive paintings in an intricate style often likened to that of Paul Klee, several dozen of which can be seen at the Fundación Pan Klub, where he had his studio. Extensively remodelled in the 1990s, the

Clockwise from left: Each level of the museum represents a stage in the work of Xul Solar; The Scorpion Mask (1953); Street in Ruins (1949); Even Zodiac Signs (1953)

museum is an exciting space on several levels, built using timber, glass and concrete. Each level represents a stage in Solar's artistic life.

Mystical art Xul Solar's preferred media were watercolours and tempera, but he also worked with composite materials to produce some of his most original works. He was interested in the occult and spent much of his life trying to invent a new religion that would end conflicts between the existing beliefs. His polychrome Pan Altars were intended to serve his universal faiths, based on an ecumenical approach. He invented Creole-based languages, too, which also creep into his paintings and their titles. One of the most unusual works is a multi-coloured musical keyboard with textured keys aimed at both the deaf and the blind.

THE BASICS

www.xulsolar.org.ar

✚ C5

✉ Laprida 1212, Recoleta

☎ 4824-3302

🕐 Tue–Fri 12–8, Sat 12–7. Closed Jan

🚇 Agüero

🚌 12, 39, 152

♿ Few

💶 Moderate

HIGHLIGHTS

● Museo Histórico
and its building
● The monument to the
foundation of Buenos Aires
● The Monumento a la
Cordialidad Internacional
● The *conventillo* mural

TIPS

● Look inside the fabulous
Iglesia Ortodoxa Rusa at
the northern side of the
park (Brasil 313). Built
in the 1890s it contains
priceless icons donated
by Tsar Nicholas II.
● Open-air concerts are
held in the colourful
amphitheatre.

This green space at the border between San
Telmo and Boca marks the spot where it all
began in the 16th century—it hosts two
historic monuments and a grove of trees.

The city's foundation This lush green area on
a gentle slope in San Telmo is where Pedro de
Mendoza may have founded Buenos Aires in
1536. In 1857, wealthy Porteño José Gregorio
Lezama bought the land, built a beautiful
mansion (now the Museo Histórico Nacional,
▷ 42–43) and planted some trees. When he
died, his widow Ángela donated the land to the
city and the park was named after her husband.
It comes into its own in the early evening,
when soft light filters through the palms and
vegetation, while children play, joggers jog and
old men play *truco*, the national card game.

A duo of monuments The over-the-top bronze and marble monument found at the northwestern corner commemorates the city's foundation. It depicts the noble Spanish conquistador overcoming the subservient native, in a rewriting of history. A more conciliatory and historically authentic monument, in the opposite corner of the park, is the Monumento a la Cordialidad Internacional (Monument to International Entente), a gift from the people of Montevideo, the Uruguayan capital. Donated in 1936, the 400th anniversary of the foundation, it is sculpted with the constellations in the sky as they were on the exact day in 1536. Opposite, at the corner of Avenida Paseo Colón and Avenida Almirante Brown, is a vivid mural depicting the *conventillos* (slum tenements) of neighbouring Boca.

THE BASICS

🚩 H10

✉ Defensa and Caseros, San Telmo

🍴 Caseros (▷ 145)

🚌 10, 24, 29, 39, 64, 130, 152

🎫 Free

HIGHLIGHTS

● Iglesia de San Pedro Telmo
● Feria de San Pedro Telmo (Sundays)
● Street tango
● Antiques shops

TIPS

● Along Calle Defensa tango soloists and orchestras vie with each other to attract crowds and sell their CDs.
● The antiques fair is safe, but as in all crowded places keep a firm grip on your belongings.

Elegant Plaza Dorrego is a quiet little square on weekdays but on weekends, especially Sunday afternoons, it buzzes with people milling between stalls selling everything from old cameras to colonial paintings.

Picturesque plaza Plaza Dorrego, one of the busiest spots in San Telmo on Sundays, is almost empty during the week, when you have a chance to admire the elegant mansions that surround it. The bars and restaurants around the square put tables on the central area, a great place to soak up the ambience. You might also like to step down Calle Humberto Primo to see the Iglesia de San Pedro Telmo, an early 18th-century Jesuit church, with its appealing eclectic facade and bell-towers capped with blue and white ceramic tiles.

Clockwise from left: Soda siphons on a stall at the Sunday Feria de San Telmo in Plaza Dorrego; locally crafted items and antiques are also on sale at the market; couples dance the tango on the plaza; browsing a prints stall; Bar Plaza Dorrego at night

Antiques The Feria de San Telmo transforms the plaza into a hive of activity on Sundays, with every square centimetre taken up by stalls selling all kinds of goods. Not all the merchandise is antique but you can find anything here from vintage vinyls and ancient gramophone players to art deco glassware and colonial oil paintings. Several stands sell fine examples of *filete*, a typical Buenos Aires art form characterized by stylized painted lettering and set-piece figures such as flowers and the Argentine flag. Equally popular are the scintillating soda siphons in every colour of the rainbow.

Tango The plaza is also a great place to see and hear tango—if you are lucky heart-throb dancer Pedro 'El Indio' Benavente will be demonstrating his skills with a pretty partner.

THE BASICS

www.feriadesantelmo.com

➕ H9

✉ Plaza Dorrego, San Telmo

🕐 Weekend markets are livelier on Sunday

🍴 Cafés, bars and restaurants all around

🚇 Independencia and San Juan

🚌 20, 59, 67, 93, 98, 126, 152

♿ Satisfactory

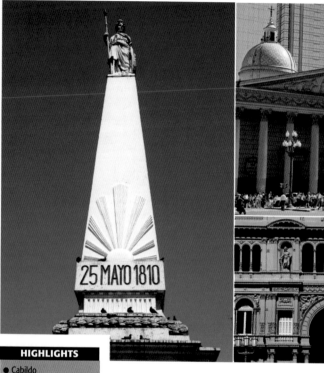

HIGHLIGHTS

● Cabildo
● Casa Rosada
● Catedral Metropolitana
(▷ 67)
● Pirámide
● Statue of Christopher
Columbus

TIPS

● Stay away from the plaza
if you see police and
protesters and come back
some other time.
● The specialized Museo
de la Casa Rosada is of
interest for big fans of
Argentine history.

Spend at least a moment or two at the
Plaza de Mayo to see the Casa Rosada—the
rosy-hued presidential palace—one of the
city's most famous sights.

Plaza from the past Named for the 1810 May
Revolution, Plaza de Mayo assumed its eclectic
appearance in the early to mid-20th century. All
that remain of the original neoclassical colon-
nade are the snow-white arches of the Cabildo,
the 18th-century government house. Inside, the
refurbished Museo Nacional del Cabildo has a
collection of city-related art and artefacts. The
plaza has seen countless political demonstrations. In 1982, crowds gathered to support the
invasion of the Malvinas/Falklands, and from
1977 to 2006 the Mothers of the Plaza de
Mayo, wearing white headscarves, patrolled the

Clockwise from far left: The Pirámide is the focus of political demonstrations; Catedral Metropolitana; the Cabildo; Casa Rosada's pinkish hue was originally created by adding ox blood to whitewash

square to draw attention to the thousands of Disappeared during the Dirty War (1976–83). The hub of demonstrations is the Pirámide, an obelisk topped by a statue of Liberty.

In the pink The plaza's crowd-pulling monument is the Casa de Gobierno (Government House), better known as the Casa Rosada (Pink House) for its colour, originally made by adding ox blood to whitewash. Eva Perón addressed adoring crowds from the balcony, most dramatically in 1951 when renouncing the vice presidency. Madonna sang 'Don't Cry for Me, Argentina' from the balcony for the 1996 biopic *Evita*. The Parque Colón (Columbus Park), the semicircular park behind the eastern facade, is dominated by a marble statue of Christopher Columbus looking back to Europe.

THE BASICS

➕ H7
✉ Plaza de Mayo, City Centre; Museo Nacional del Cabildo: Bolívar 65
☎ Museo Nacional del Cabildo: 4334-1782
🕐 Museo Nacional del Cabildo: Tue–Fri 11.30–6 Sat–Sun 2–6
🍴 Cafés, bars and restaurants along Avenida de Mayo and Calle Florida
🚇 Plaza de Mayo, Catedral, Bolívar
🚌 28, 56, 105, 126
♿ Satisfactory
🎫 Museo Nacional del Cabildo: inexpensive

HIGHLIGHTS

● The trees
● Torre de los Ingleses
● The San Martín monument
● Palacio San Martín and Palacio Retiro

TIPS

● Both *palacios* run guided visits in Spanish or English.
● Timetables are posted outside.
● Climb the Torre de los Ingleses for the great views.
● The Plaza is great for a picnic—stock up at the Disco supermarket (Esmeralda 1365).

Compact Retiro can breathe thanks to this lovely green space between the city centre, the port and the main commuter terminals. An imposing equestrian statue of independence hero José de San Martín recalls the Liberator the square is named after.

Respite in Retiro Landscaped by Frenchman Charles Thays (▷ 32), this majestic plaza is a botanical centrepiece for the patrician *barrio* of Retiro. Its grassy lawns and shaded benches are favoured by office workers, while the indigo-blossomed jacarandas and a venerable rubber tree *(gomero)* form a handsome backdrop for the fine bronze of San Martín himself, by French sculptor Louis-Joseph Daumas. The plaza was renamed in 1878, the centenary of his birth, in the Liberator's honour. At the northern end, the

Clockwise from left: Palacio Retiro is also known as Palacio Paz after its first owner, José Paz; a sweeping staircase in Palacio San Martín; the Torre de los Ingleses; arms and armour at the Museo de Armas; an exterior view of Palacio Retiro; trees shade the plaza

Torre de los Ingleses (Tower of the English), vaguely reminiscent of the Big Ben tower, was a 1910 centenary gift to the nation from the Anglo-Argentine community. The nearby monument to Argentina's Malvinas/Falkland fallen is solemnly guarded by the military.

Panoply of palaces Striking Palacio Retiro and elegant Palacio San Martín were built in the first decade of the 20th century. Media mogul José Paz and heiress Mercedes Castellanos de Anchorena wanted their homes to look like Parisian *palais*. The former opted for a Louvre-Versailles combo while the Palacio San Martín is modelled partly on the Hôtel de Condé. Palacio Retiro (also known as Palacio Paz) is now an officers' club, while Palacio San Martín is the official home of the Foreign Ministry.

THE BASICS

➕ G5

✉ Plaza San Martín, Retiro. Palacio Retiro: Avenida Santa Fe 750; Palacio San Martín: Arenales and Esmeralda

☎ Palacio Retiro: 4311-1071; Palacio San Martín: 4819-9092

🎫 Palacio Retiro: guided visits in English, Wed and Thu 3.30; Palacio San Martín: visits Thu 11, Fri 3, 4, 5

🍴 Cafés and restaurants on Avenida Santa Fe and Calle Florida

🚇 San Martín

🚌 10, 17, 152

♿ Satisfactory

💰 Moderate

- Ethnic rugs at Arte Étnico Argentino
- Shoes at Mishka's
- Great bags at Humawaca

TIPS

- Most boutiques are open only in the afternoon—some close on Monday but many open on Sunday.
- Local hotels and other establishments dish out free maps of the *barrio* with shops and outlets clearly marked.
- Check your Argentine sizes—though most assistants will soon size you up.

Palermo Soho is a great place to shop, thanks to a bewildering array of little boutiques where you can get Argentine leather bags, ethnic carpets, tango CDs and plenty more.

Designer delights Start at the Plaza Serrano, Palermo Soho's hub: You might find what you're looking for right away, as the square bristles with stalls selling crafts. Head west along Honduras, and Papelera Palermo (▷ 126) might entice you with its fine stationery and unique albums. Calma Chicha (▷ 122), just a paperweight's throw along the same street, has great modern design items, some made from Argentine cowhide. Opposite, on the corner with Gurruchaga, is one of the city's leading record shops, Miles (▷ 125).

VIsitors to the city are delighted to find so many small and not-so-small individual shops in Palermo Soho

Turn left down Gurruchaga and you'll reach Juana de Arco's clothing and lingerie boutique (▷ 124) at the corner of El Salvador. Then turn right and the next corner can offer a break; Mark's Deli (▷ 147) is a great place to linger over a cup of fruit tea.

More delights A few yards along El Salvador, Humawaca (▷ 124) is great for leather goods. The divine textiles at Arte Étnico Argentino (▷ 121) are irresistible, though the prices reflect the high quality. By now you might have worn out your shoe leather, so step back to the corner with Armenia and you will find some comfortable but stylish footwear at Mishka's. At the corner of El Salvador and Gurruchaga pop into El Cid (▷ 122) for a floral shirt–and perhaps book a dinner at Freud y Fahler (▷ 146).

THE BASICS

➕ A4
✉ Plaza Serrano and around, Palermo
🍴 Cafés, bars and restaurants
🚇 Plaza Italia
🚌 15, 39, 55, 60, 93, 152
♿ Satisfactory

HIGHLIGHTS

● The exterior
● Performances
● Salón Dorado

TIPS

● Guided visits take in the costume and set workshops plus the sumptuous auditorium.
● Non-residents are charged more for tickets than residents, so try to go with a local to get around this discrimination.

One of the greatest opera houses in the world, no less, this magnificent concert hall has echoed to all the great divas and maestros since it was inaugurated in 1908.

Pride and joy The Teatro Colón (Columbus Theatre), one of the world's superlative classical music venues, knocks other buildings on the Avenida 9 de Julio (▷ 14–15) into second place. Its first architect, Tamburini, laid the cornerstone in 1889 with his fellow Italian pupil Meano, who later took over the project, but both were dead within 15 years, leaving the finishing touches to Belgian architect Jules Dormal, who added sober Gallic elements to the Italianate exterior. The theatre was inaugurated in 1908 for a performance of Verdi's *Aida*. Following lengthy renovation it reopened amid

For more than 100 years, this stunning venue has welcomed the leading operatic performers and attracted audiences from far and wide

much jubilation on 24 May 2010, on the eve of Argentina's bicentenary celebrations.

Operatic opulence The list of names of the opera singers and ballet dancers, composers and conductors who have appeared here reads like a history of classical music. Stravinsky and Strauss, Joan Sutherland and Plácido Domingo have all performed here, as have home-grown stars like Daniel Barenboim and Julio Bocca. Ranked in the world's top five venues for acoustics, the Colón is also one of the biggest, with a capacity exceeding 3,500. The neo-Renaissance interior features a magnificent marble staircase and Salón Dorado (Golden Hall), inspired by Versailles. The auditorium's rich decor is set off by the delicate 1960s frescoes in the huge dome, the work of Argentine artist, Raúl Soldi.

THE BASICS

www.teatrocolon.org.ar

➕ F6

✉ Cerrito 618, City Centre

☎ 5533-5599

🎭 Check website for individual performances

🍴 Bar in theatre

🚇 Tribunales

🚌 10, 17, 29

♿ Good

✋ Guided visits: moderate

HIGHLIGHTS

● The subtropical
vegetation
● Launch trips
● Outdoor activities,
including kayaking
● Museo de Arte del Tigre
● Parque de la Costa

TIPS

● In summer, people bathe
in Tigre's waterways—the
water is surprisingly clean
and refreshingly cool.
● As you might expect in
a warm, watery place,
mosquitoes are rampant on
summer evenings, so take
lots of repellent.

This subtropical settlement crouches by the
Paraná delta, a fan of fertile earth and vegetation carried down the river from tropical
Brazil. Water is the leitmotif—travel the
channels in wooden launches or go rowing
or kayaking through the maze of creeks.

Tiger on the banks Just north of Buenos Aires,
languid El Tigre (named for the wild felines that
once prowled here) guards the Paraná delta at
the head of the Río de la Plata, a soothingly
green landscape of wooded islands, separated
by a labyrinth of waterways plied by picturesque
wooden launches. Its heyday was the early
20th century, when its famous casino was a
playground for wealthy Porteños, but it fell out
of favour in the 1950s when they began to
travel further afield for their summer holidays,

Clockwise from left: *The Museo de Arte del Tigre is housed in a superb former casino building; a boardwalk path through the Tres Boca neighbourhood; people enjoying the dusk in El Tigre; a popcorn and sweet stall; a passenger boat cruises the delta*

and gambling was banned. Tigre's main attractions include a wide range of water sports.

Fun for all the family The sumptuous Museo de Arte del Tigre, or MAT, is housed in a splendid French-style edifice, overlooking one of the main waterways. Argentina's first casino when it opened in 1912, it stood derelict for decades until it was finally turned into an art gallery. The centrepiece former ballroom houses Argentine paintings related to portside life, including works by Boca maestro Quinquela Martín (▷ 73). By contrast, the Parque de la Costa is one of the largest theme parks in Latin America. At the confluence of the ríos Tigre and Luján, right next to the Estación Delta, it offers all manner of attractions and rides, including some dramatic roller-coasters *(montañas rusas)*.

THE BASICS

www.parquedelacosta.com.ar
www.mat.gov.ar
✚ Off map to north
✉ Parque de la Costa: Vivanco 1509
MAT: Paseo Victorica 972
☎ Parque: 4002-6000; MAT: 4512-4528
🕐 Parque de la Costa: Apr–Nov Sat–Sun 11–7; Dec–Mar Tue–Sun 11–9. MAT: Wed–Fri 9–7, Sat–Sun 12–7; guided tours every hour
🚆 Suburban line from Retiro (▷ 92–97) or the tourist Tren de la Costa to Estación Fluvial, where you can catch public launches run by three companies: Delta, Interisleña and Jilgüero. An excellent option is the four-hour round trip to the Paraná de las Palmas.
♿ Poor
✋ Parque de la Costa: expensive.
MAT: inexpensive

More to See

This section contains other great places to visit if you have more time. Some are in the heart of the city while others are a short journey away, found under Further Afield.

In the Heart of the City

BARRIO PARQUE

This leafy park, also known as Palermo Chico, laid out by French landscape gardener Charles Thays (▷ 32), hosts ambassadorial residences and embassies, alongside villas and mansions. Architectural styles range from mock-Tudor to Flemish Renaissance, and art deco to Secessionist.

🚩 D3 ✉ Calle Ombú and around, Palermo
🚌 10, 37, 59, 60, 92

BASÍLICA DEL SANTÍSIMO SACRAMENTO

Modelled on Sacré-Coeur in Paris, this majestic church, inaugurated in 1916, was carefully renovated in 2007, when its white marble cupola and svelte towers were scrubbed clean. Heiress Mercedes Castellanos de Anchorena spared no expense on the interior: She imported French bronze, Venetian tiles, Carrara marble and Moroccan onyx to create a masterpiece, set off by the neo-Byzantine altarpiece and Flemish confessionals.

🚩 G5 ✉ San Martín 1039, Retiro
🚇 San Martín 🚌 10, 17, 152 🎫 Free

BASÍLICA DE NUESTRA SEÑORA DEL PILAR

Next to Recoleta cemetery is the city's most appealing colonial church. Plain white externally, the basilica, consecrated in 1732, is finely decorated inside—the high-point is a baroque silver altarpiece from Peru. You can visit the cloisters to see colonial silverware.

🚩 E4 ✉ Junín 1904, Recoleta ☎ 4803-6793 🕐 Mon–Sat 10.30–6.15, Sun 2.30–6.15; guided visits in Spanish most Sun at 3 🚌 10, 17, 60, 67, 92, 110 🎫 Free

CALLE DEFENSA

Within San Telmo, Calle Defensa, named after the defence of the city from the British (▷ 10), is lined with boutiques and antiques shops. South of Plaza Dorrego is the late-19th-century Pasaje de la Defensa shopping arcade; initially inhabited by one clan, it was later home to 32 families. One block north is the superb Mercado Municipal (▷ 125, panel).

🚩 H9 ✉ Calle Defensa, San Telmo
🚇 Independencia and San Juan
🚌 20, 59, 67, 93, 98, 126, 152

A villa in wealthy Barrio Parque

Basílica del Santísimo Sacramento

CALLE FLORIDA

Joining Plaza de Mayo (▷ 54–55) in the heart of downtown to Plaza San Martín (▷ 56–57) in chic Retiro, pedestrianized Calle Florida is the best-known and most-frequented shopping street in the city. Be prepared for a headlong onslaught of small shops and cluttered kiosks, old-fashioned galleries and medium-sized department stores. The street itself is alive with persuasive vendors, scantily clad girls handing out flyers and the occasional human statue. Pairs of tango dancers strut their stuff, often pulling in 'volunteers'.

🔒 G6 ✉ Calle Florida, City Centre 🚇 Florida/San Martín 🚌 6, 50, 62, 74, 115, 130, 140, 152, 195

CATEDRAL ANGLICANA

www.catedralanglicana.com
The country's main Anglican church, the Catedral Anglicana de San Juan Bautista (inaugurated in 1831) is proof of the important role played by the Anglo-Argentine community in the city's history: Sunday services in English have been celebrated here since the 1830s. The facade is that of a sober Roman temple with six columns, while inside the altar is decorated with intriguing wooden objects crafted by indigenous peoples from the far-off Chaco region.

🔒 H7 ✉ 25 de Mayo 276, City Centre 🚇 Leandro N. Alem 🚌 28, 50

CATEDRAL METROPOLITANA

www.catedralbuenosaires.com
Plans to build the cathedral began in the 1810s, but the construction of the neoclassical building, with a sober facade inspired by the Palais Bourbon in Paris, dragged on until 1863. Argentines head for the mausoleum of General San Martín: The marble monument is by French sculptor, Albert Carrier-Belleuse, and the sarcophagus is symbolically protected by three female allegories of Argentina, Chile and Peru, all liberated by San Martín from Spanish rule.

🔒 H7 ✉ Rivadavia and San Martín, City Centre ☎ 4331-2845 🕐 Mon–Fri 8–7, Sat–Sun 9–7.30 🚇 Plaza de Mayo, Catedral, Bolívar 🚌 24, 64, 130

Shoppers on pedestrianized Calle Florida

Inside the Catedral Metropolitana

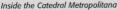

CENTRO CULTURAL RECOLETA (CCR)

www.centroculturalrecoleta.org

Along from the Basílica del Pilar (▷ 66) is the Centro Cultural Recoleta. It is part of the Franciscan monastery that gave the *barrio* of Recoleta its name (the monks had settled there in the early 18th century to meditate or 'recollect' their thoughts) and was remodelled in the 1980s to make way for this avant-garde facility. The centre showcases contemporary painting and sculpture, photography and theatre, dance and other performance arts.

🔳 E4 ⊠ Junín 1930, Recoleta ☎ 4803-1040 ⏰ Tue–Fri 2–9, Sat–Sun 10–9 🚇 10, 17, 60, 67, 92, 110 ♿ Few 🎟 Inexpensive

EDIFICIO BAROLO

www.pbarolo.com.ar

The Edificio Barolo—known as Palacio Barolo or Pasaje Barolo—added its unusual profile to the Buenos Aires skyline in 1923. At 100m (328ft), including the beacon on the top, it was the tallest building in South America for 12 years, until the Kavanagh building in Retiro usurped that record. It gets its name from Luis Barolo, a highly successful sheep farmer, woollens exporter and Dante fanatic, who commissioned Italian architect Mario Palanti to design it. Exotically eclectic in style, it is fascinating for the allegorical references to Dante's *Divine Comedy*: There are 22 floors, the number of stanzas in each canto, while its height in metres (100) is the same as the number of cantos.

🔳 F7 ⊠ Avenida de Mayo 1370, City Centre ☎ 4381-1885 ⏰ Guided visits on Mon and Thu 4–7 🚇 Congreso 🚌 12, 37, 64, 86 ♿ None 🎟 Guided visits: moderate

ESTACIÓN FERROVIARIO RETIRO

The city's major commuter railway station—actually a trio of terminals—the Estación Ferroviario Retiro is also a national monument and is regarded as one of the finest buildings of its kind in the world. Inaugurated in 1915, it was designed by four British architects and engineers. Its impressive steel

The view over Plaza del Congreso from Edificio Barolo

skeleton was manufactured in Liverpool and reassembled *in situ*. If you use the Mitre terminal (the one nearest to Plaza San Martín) to get to Belgrano or El Tigre, take some time to admire the French-style facade, with its harmonious colonnades and majestic cupola. Art nouveau Royal Doulton porcelain wall- and ceiling-tiles enhance the vast interior's opulent elegance, not least in the station's Café Retiro, with its stained-glass dome, polished woodwork and gleaming chandeliers.

➕ G5 ✉ Plaza San Martín, Retiro
🚇 San Martín, Retiro 🚌 10, 17, 152
♿ Good

FLORALIS GENÉRICA

Installed in 2002—a gift from architect and designer Eduardo Catalano to a city emerging from crisis—the giant metallic flower, 25m (82ft) tall, known as *Floralis Genérica,* has already become one of Buenos Aires' most recognizable icons. Its six shiny petals, reflected in a giant pool at the centre of the Plaza Naciones Unidas, open and close every morning at 8am and evening at sunset, thanks to an impressive system of light sensors and hydraulics. It is open 24 hours on 25 May (Independence Day), 21 September (first day of spring), Christmas Eve and New Year's Eve.

➕ E3 ✉ Plaza de la Naciones Unidas, Recoleta 🚌 17, 62, 67, 93, 130

FUNDACIÓN KLEMM

www.fundacionfjklemm.org
Federico Jorge Klemm (1942–2002), a larger-than-life artist who openly modelled himself on Andy Warhol, collected and sponsored art, and produced some wildly original works of his own. He set up his own foundation for one of the most important private collections in Argentina, housed in a plain, modern building overlooking the Plaza San Martín. It includes pieces by Picasso and Man Ray, plus some by leading Argentine artists such as Guillermo Kuitca and Antonio Berni.

➕ G6 ✉ Marcelo T. de Alvear 626, Retiro
☎ 4312-4443 🕐 Mon–Fri 11–8 🚇 San Martín 🚌 10, 17, 152 ♿ Few 🎫 Free

A work in Fundación Klemm

Floralis Genérica by Eduardo Catalano

FUNDACIÓN PROA

www.proa.org

An Italianate mansion and a sleek contemporary building next door house one of the city's most creative spaces, the Fundación PROA. At the cutting-edge of world art, the PROA has undertaken exciting projects, including illuminating the iconic transporter bridge across the Riachuelo. Exhibitions focus on Argentine and Latin American art.
🔁 J12 ✉ Avenida Pedro de Mendoza 1929, Boca ☎ 4104-1000 ⏰ Tue–Sun 11–7 🚌 20, 25, 29, 53, 64, 152 ♿ Good 🎫 Free

HIPÓDROMO ARGENTINO DE PALMERO

www.palermo.com.ar

All things equestrian have a huge following in Argentina and this national racetrack does the country proud. Founded in the late 19th century, the racing club has an early 20th-century beaux-arts grandstand. The main building was designed by Louis Faure-Dujarric and inaugurated in 1908.
🔁 A1 ✉ Avenida del Libertador 4101, Palermo ☎ 4778-2800 ⏰ Check website for race times 🚇 Palermo/Ministro Carranza 🚌 10, 34, 130, 160, 166 ♿ Good

JARDÍN ZOOLÓGICO

www.zoobuenosaires.com.ar

Like so many outdoor sights in Buenos Aires, the zoo was designed by the prolific Charles Thays. Restored at the end of the 20th century this fine zoo now offers an agreeable experience for its inmates and visitors alike. Many of the buildings are architectural wonders in themselves, modelled on Indian temples and Japanese pagodas. The fauna includes native species such as penguins and llamas, while the Himalayan snow leopards draw in the crowds.
🔁 B3 ✉ Avenida Sarmiento and Avenida Las Heras, Palermo ☎ 4011-9900 ⏰ Tue–Sun 10–7 (last tickets sold at 6) 🚇 Plaza Italia 🚌 10, 29, 34, 60, 111, 118, 152, 160, 188 ♿ Good 🎫 Moderate

LIBRERÍA DE ÁVILA

www.libreriadeavila.servisur.com

There has been a bookshop on this corner of Alsina and Bolívar, opposite San Ignacio church, since

A horse race at the Hipódromo

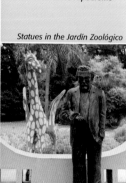

Statues in the Jardín Zoológico

1785; they say that this is where the first book was sold in the city. Porteños are avid readers and there are dozens of bookshops around the city, but the Librería de Ávila is the oldest one still trading, though the building has undergone extensive renovation.
🚩 H8 ✉ Alsina 500, City Centre
☎ 4331-8989 🚇 Perú, Plaza de Mayo
🚌 2, 23, 91, 98 ♿ Few

LUNA PARK
www.lunapark.com.ar
With 7,000 seats and 70 years of history, the art deco Luna Park stadium is a great landmark of downtown Buenos Aires. This is where Carlos Gardel's funeral (▷ 73) and General Perón's first meeting with Evita took place. Over the years it has hosted world-stopping boxing matches, audiences with Pope John Paul II, concerts by Jethro Tull, Frank Sinatra, Lily Allen and Boy George, world volleyball championships, *Holiday on Ice* and ballet spectacles. Be sure to book a seat with a view of the stage.

🚩 H6 ✉ Avenida Madero 420, City Centre
☎ 4311-1990 🕐 See website for concerts and shows 🚇 Alem 🚌 4, 6, 20, 152
♿ Good

MANZANA FRANCISCANA
The Franciscan Order has always played a key part in the city's history and it was allocated this downtown *manzana* (block) as soon as Buenos Aires was founded in 1580. The original mud-brick buildings were replaced by stone in the 18th century. The complex is dominated by the Basílica de San Francisco and the Capilla de San Roque, outstanding for its German-style neo-baroque facade. Part of the austerely beautiful Convento de San Francisco, next door, is the small Museo Monseñor Bottaro with a number of interesting items on display, including a time capsule buried in the basilica in 1908.

🚩 H8 ✉ City Centre 🕐 Basílica de San Francisco and Capilla de San Roque Mon–Sat 9–5. Museo Monseñor Bottaro daily 10–4 🚇 Plaza de Mayo 🚌 24, 29, 126
♿ Few 🎟 Inexpensive

A corner of the facade of Luna Park, Buenos Aires' landmark stadium

MERCADO DE ABASTO

www.abasto-shopping.com.ar

Dating from the late 19th century as the main market, this current building is an art deco masterpiece from the 1930s. It continued as the main fresh produce market until the 1980s. The fabulous shell, with its majestic arches and impressive vaulted roofs, was then reinvented as one of the city's biggest shopping malls. In addition to shops, there is a cinema, a kosher McDonald's, a wide variety of other eateries and a highly commercial but fun museum for children.

🚩 C6 ✉ Avenida Corrientes 3247, Abasto ☎ 4959-3400 🕐 Daily 10–10. Food patio: Sun–Thu 10am–midnight, Fri–Sat and day before hols 10am–2am 🍴 Food patio 🚇 Carlos Gardel 🚌 24, 26, 29, 62, 64, 110, 188 ♿ Good

MONUMENTO DE LOS ESPAÑOLES

One of the city's landmarks and a majestic outdoor sculpture, the Spaniards' Monument stands at the middle of a busy roundabout, where Avenidas del Libertador and Sarmiento cross. This art nouveau wonder of white Carrara marble represents the Magna Carta, Argentina's mid-19th-century constitution, with a mass of allegorical figures topped by an angel. The four bronzes at its feet represent the major regions of the country.

🚩 C2 ✉ Avenida del Libertador/Avenida Sarmiento, Palermo 🚌 34, 67, 130

MUSEO DE ARTE POPULAR JOSÉ HERNÁNDEZ

www.museohernandez.org.ar

Most of the art on display in Buenos Aires is European either in origin or in influence, so it is refreshing to find somewhere that unashamedly displays traditional Argentine arts and crafts. This collection of popular *criollo* artefacts is housed in a neoclassical Italianate mansion and its various outbuildings. There is silverware, plenty of interesting textiles and no end of *mate* receptacles.

🚩 D3 ✉ Avenida del Libertador 2373, Palermo ☎ 4803-2384 🕐 Wed–Fri 1–7, Sat–Sun 10–8 🚌 10, 37, 59, 60, 92 ♿ Few 🎫 Inexpensive; Sun free

Abasto shopping mall is housed in the shell of a former market building

Monumento de los Españoles

MUSEO DE ARTES PLÁSTICAS EDUARDO SÍVORI

www.museosivori.org.ar

One of Parque Tres de Febrero's delights is this elegant collection of Argentine plastic arts, in a well-arranged modern building amid the park's greenery. One of the oils on display is a delicate portrait of a Porteño woman (*Dama porteña*) by 19th-century master Prilidiano Pueyrredón. There are also fine sculptures, and one or two Uruguayan artists are represented.

➕ B1 ✉ Avenida Infanta Isabel 555 and Libertador, Palermo ☎ 4774-9452 🕐 Tue–Fri 12–8, Sat–Sun 10–8 🍴 Café 🚌 34, 67, 130 ♿ Good 🎫 Inexpensive, Wed, Sat free

MUSEO DE BELLAS ARTES DE LA BOCA

To see paintings by local hero Quinquela Martín, look no further than this museum, built on the site of his studio. Abandoned in a convent and adopted by a poor Boquense couple, Martín was dis-covered by President Marcelo T. de Alvear and shot to fame. Other works are on permanent display in the Museo Nacional de Bellas Artes (▷ 46–47) as well as Paris, London and Rome. The vigorous oils focus on the shipyards and factories of his home *barrio*.

➕ J12 ✉ Pedro de Mendoza 1835, Boca ☎ 4301-1497 🕐 Tue–Fri 10.30–5.30, Sat–Sun 11–5.30 🚌 29, 53, 64, 152 ♿ Few 🎫 Free

MUSEO CASA CARLOS GARDEL

www.museocasacarlosgardel.buenosaires. gob.ar

Carlos Gardel (died 1935), the world's greatest tango singer, made this town house his home in the 1920s. Since 2003 it has been a museum and a tribute to this Argentine hero. Some rooms, have been restored. Film screenings (Gardel was a movie idol), and recitals of the songs that made the 'Creole Thrush' such a star, are held regularly.

➕ C6 ✉ Jean Jaurés 735, Abasto ☎ 4964-2015 🕐 Mon, Wed–Fri 11–6, Sat–Sun, hols 10–7 🚇 Carlos Gardel 🚌 29, 41, 64, 68, 118, 140, 142, 168, 188 ♿ Few 🎫 Inexpensive (Wed free)

A Carlos Gardel mural on window shutters near the museum dedicated to him

MUSEO DE LA CIUDAD

www.museodelaciudad.buenosaires.gov.ar

The city museum, in the 1894 Casa de los Querubines, stages exhibitions about Buenos Aires. Its collection covers everything from vintage toys and early photographs to old furniture and *fileteado*—a Porteño art form: stylized lettering and images painted on to objects, such as buses or signs.

🔢 H8 ✉ Defensa 219, City centre ☎ 4331-9855 🕙 Daily 11–7 🚇 Plaza de Mayo, Bolívar, Catedral 🚌 24, 29, 126 ♿ Few 💰 Inexpensive (Mon, Wed free)

PALACIO DE LAS AGUAS CORRIENTES

This hulk of a building, whose name translates as 'Palace of Running Waters' occupies a whole block in the Balvanera *barrio*. Designed in the late 19th century by Swedish-Argentine architect Carlos Nyströmer and Norwegian engineer Olaf Boye, its style is basically French neo-Renaissance, evidenced by the steep mansard roofs. Thanks to a coating of more than 300,000 bluish-green Royal Doulton ceramic tiles and terra-cotta bricks, it resembles an extravagant Victorian town hall. Inside are pumps and all manner of water-related machinery plus vintage WCs and bidets.

🔢 E6 ✉ Avenida Córdoba 1950, City Centre ☎ 3479-0105 🕙 Mon–Fri 9–12 🚇 Callao, Facultad de Medicina 🚌 60, 86, 168 ♿ Few 💰 Free

PALACIO DEL CONGRESO NACIONAL

www.congreso.gov.ar

The building housing Argentina's national parliament, the Palacio del Congreso Nacional, is a great bastion of grey granite, dominating the Plaza del Congreso at the western end of Avenida de Mayo (▷ 16–17). Atop the palatial Academic edifice soars the Greco-Roman cupola, 80m (262ft) in height and visible from much of the city. One of the most impressive details inside is a two-tonne bronze and crystal chandelier, decorated with figures representing Argentina and all its provinces.

🔢 E7 ✉ Hipólito Irigoyen 1846, City Centre

The Palacio del Congreso Nacional

☎ 6310-7222 🚫 Closed Jan and during session; English visits Mon, Tue, Thu and Fri 11 and 4 🚇 Congreso (A) 🚌 12, 37, 60 ♿ Few 🎫 Free

PALAIS DE GLACE

www.palaisdeglace.gob.ar

Officially called Palacio Nacional de las Artes, the Palais de Glace (originally a skating-rink) is an unusual circular belle-époque building used mainly for art exhibitions and trade shows. It is said to be where tango finally became socially acceptable in the 1920s thanks to soirées held by the Barón de Marchi. Every June the Palais de Glace hosts the Sala Nacional de Artes Visuales, an expo of visual arts that focuses on photography. There are regular tango shows plus cinema showings at weekends.

➕ F4 ✉ Posadas 1725, Recoleta ☎ 4804-4324 🚫 Tue–Fri 12–8, Sat–Sun 10–8 🚌 17, 61, 67, 92, 130 ♿ Few 🎫 Free

PALERMO VIEJO

The core of Buenos Aires' biggest *barrio* is known as Palermo Viejo, 'Old Palermo'. Many of its single-floor neoclassical mansions have been converted into lodgings, boutiques, bars and restaurants, making it one of the most attractive areas to visit. Cobbled streets, shady plane-trees, the community feel and laid-back atmosphere all add to the attraction. Railway tracks shear the sub-*barrio* in half, the southern realms dubbed 'Soho' in reference to the trendy New York neighbourhood, while the northern part is called 'Hollywood' with its TV studios and art galleries.

➕ B4 ✉ Around Plaza Serrano, Palermo 🚇 Plaza Italia, Palermo, Ministro Carranza 🚌 39, 55, 60, 64, 67, 93, 152

PASAJE SAN LORENZO Y EL ZANJÓN

www.elzanjon.com.ar

Visits to El Zanjón de Granados, or simply, El Zanjón (the Ditch), offer an interesting insight into the city's 18th-century foundations. Guided tours negotiate a maze of brick-lined underground passages and water pipes. At ground level, the photogenic Pasaje San Lorenzo is an alleyway of typical San Telmo

Outdoor tables at a restaurant in Plaza Serrano

The Palais de Glace is used for exhibitions and trade shows

houses, including the Casa Mínima at No. 380, barely 2m (2 yards) wide, which can be visited via the Zanjón, as part of organized visits to the underground passages.

➕ H9 ✉ Defensa 755, San Telmo ☎ 4361-3002 🕐 Zanjón: Mon–Fri 11–4, Sun 1–6, 1-hour tours. Casa Mínima: Mon–Fri 10.30–4, half-hour tours (reserve in advance) 🚌 24, 93, 130, 152 ♿ Few 💲 Moderate

PLANETARIO GALILEO GALILEI

www.planetario.gov.ar

At the eastern tip of Parque Tres de Febrero, this planetarium resembles a flying-saucer with a globe on top. The 1960s building is a fun place to find out about the solar system. Some aspects are alarming, not least the huge meteorites: One weighs more than 1,500kg (3,300lbs) but is a mere stripling compared with 'El Chaco', which fell on to northern Argentina about 4,000 years ago.

➕ G1 ✉ Avenida Sarmiento and Belisario Roldán, Palermo ☎ 4771-9393 🕐 Mon–Fri 9–6, Sat–Sun 2.30–9 🚌 34, 67, 130 ♿ Few 💲 Free; shows: Moderate

PLAZA CARLOS PELLEGRINI

This tiny triangle in Retiro is named for a late 19th-century president who founded the Jockey Club here. The club's headquarters are in the Palacio Unzué de Casares, an Academic-style mansion. Opposite is the Palacio Celedonio Pereda, a replica Parisian *palais* and the Brazilian ambassador's residence. A marble statue of Pellegrini stands on the plaza.

➕ F5 ✉ Retiro 🚇 San Martín 🚌 55, 60, 64, 67, 93, 152

PREDIO LA RURAL

www.la-rural.com.ar

This major venue epitomizes the bond between the capital and its rural hinterland. The complex, built in the early 20th century, hosts the Exposición de Ganadería, Agricultura e Industria (▷ 162). Also on the premises is the Ópera Pampa, an entertainment with gaucho displays and folk music.

➕ B3 ✉ Avenida Santa Fe 4363, Palermo ☎ 4324-4700 🕐 See website for shows, times and prices 🚇 Plaza Italia 🚌 39, 59, 60, 152 ♿ Good

Flying-saucer shaped Planetario Galileo Galilei is in Parque Tres de Febrero

Visit Casa Mínima on tours of El Zanjón

Further Afield

CEMENTERIO DE LA CHACARITA

www.cementeriochacarita.com.ar
Overshadowed by La Recoleta
(▷ 24–25), the vast Chacarita
graveyard was created in the
1870s. The biggest draw is the
tomb of tango giant Carlos Gardel.
✚ Page 112 ✉ Guzmán 630 and Federico
Lacroze, Chacarita ☎ 4553-9034 ◷ Daily
7-6 🚇 Federico Lacroze 🚌 39, 42, 44, 47,
63, 111, 112, 127 ♿ Good 🎟 Free

FERIA DE MATADEROS

www.feriademataderos.com.ar
Created in 1986, the lively Feria
de las Artesanías y Tradiciones
Populares Argentinas (Fair for
Argentina's Popular Arts, Crafts
and Traditions) revived the *criollo*
culture in the capital. On most
weekends (usually Sundays),
streets near a livestock market in
the *barrio* of Mataderos come alive
with folk music and gaucho antics.
✚ Page 112 ✉ Lisandro de la Torre,
Mataderos ☎ 4687-5602 ◷ Apr–Nov Sun
11am–sunset; closed Mar, Dec–Feb Sat
🍴 Street food including barbecues 🚌 55,
80, 92, 126, 180, 185 ♿ Good 🎟 Free

MUSEO ARGENTINO DE CIENCIAS NATURALES

www.macn.secyt.gov.ar
The natural history museum
occupies an art deco masterpiece.
Its collections are remarkable—
Argentina has some of the world's
biggest and best dinosaur remains.
✚ Page 113 ✉ Avenida Ángel Gallardo
470, Villa Crespo ☎ 4982-6595 ◷ Daily
2–7 (closed some holidays) 🚇 Ángel
Gallardo 🚌 15, 55, 65, 99, 105, 141 ♿ Few
🎟 Inexpensive

MUSEO DE ARTE ESPAÑOL

www.museolarreta.buenosaires.gob.ar
This Andalucian-style mansion was
built at the beginning of the 20th
century for Uruguayan Enrique
Larreta. Living in Spain from 1900
to 1916, Larreta amassed paintings and furniture, plus a shipload
of silverware and porcelain. When
he died in 1961, his collections
were bequeathed to the city.
✚ Page 112 ✉ Juramento 2291, Belgrano
☎ 4784-4040 ◷ Mon–Fri 2–8, Sat–Sun,
hols 10–8 🍴 Nearby cafés and restaurants
🚇 Juramento 🚌 44, 55, 60, 80, 114, 118
♿ Few 🎟 Inexpensive (Thu free)

The Feria de Mataderos brings gauchos to the barrio

City Tours

This section contains self-guided tours that will help you explore the sights in each of the city's regions. Each tour is designed to take a day, with a map pinpointing the recommended places along the way. There is a quick reference guide at the end of each tour, listing everything you need in that region, so you know exactly what's close by.

CITY TOURS

City Centre

With its grand avenues and historic *manzanas* (blocks), the middle of Buenos Aires is packed with eye-catching buildings—a world-class opera house, the rosy-hued presidential palace and a luxurious shopping arcade. Don't expect much peace or quiet (except on Sunday)—this is where the city does its business.

Morning
Kick off your tour of the *microcentro*, as locals call the **City Centre**, with a caffeine boost at **Café Tortoni** (▷ 144)—admittedly a touristy place but divine nonetheless. Then you should be ready to explore the length of **Avenida de Mayo** (▷ 16–17), ideal for a morning stroll.

Mid-morning
You could first head eastwards to **Plaza de Mayo** (▷ 54–55), which forms one end of the great avenue. Here you can tick off one of the city's major sights, the pink Casa Rosada (presidential palace), and at least glimpse the austere **Catedral Metropolitana** (▷ 67) and the whitewashed Cabildo, or colonial government house.

Now head back in the opposite direction, remembering to look skywards to take in the ornate roofs and architectural detailing. After five blocks you will cross the great **Avenida 9 de Julio** (▷ 14–15)—look right for a view of the iconic El Obelisco. Now try to make it to **Palacio del Congreso Nacional** (▷ 74) by 11am for a tour of Argentina's parliament building. The *subte* (metro) or a stroll along Avenida Callao will get you to wherever you decide to have lunch.

Lunch
On weekdays opportunities for lunch abound, as you can join office workers for a quick snack or dine more leisurely in a restaurant or *confitería*. **Parrilla Peña** (▷ 148) stands out for its exceptional steak while organic and veggie **Granix** (▷ 147), in the sumptuous **Galería Güemes** (▷ 124), offers a respite from meat eating.

Afternoon

Window-shopping is made easy—and into an art form—at the elegant **Galerías Pacífico** (▷ 30–31). Maybe have another coffee or an ice cream downstairs at the **Centro Cultural Borges** (▷ 134)—or check out a temporary art exhibition upstairs.

Mid-afternoon

Now it is time for some more culture at the historical **Manzana de las Luces** (▷ 34–35; right). Most tours begin around 4pm but if you want an English-speaking guide you will need to contact them two weeks in advance.

Evening

Buy opera or ballet tickets for a night to remember at the **Teatro Colón** (▷ 60–61; left), or for folk, rock or tango music try to get seats at the **ND/Ateneo** (▷ 136). If you want to eat beforehand, a *confitería* such as **Florida Garden** (▷ 146) might be a good bet.

Dinner

If taking your time over exquisitely prepared food with excellent service is more your idea of a great evening out, try **Tomo 1** (▷ 151)—but book a table to avoid disappointment.

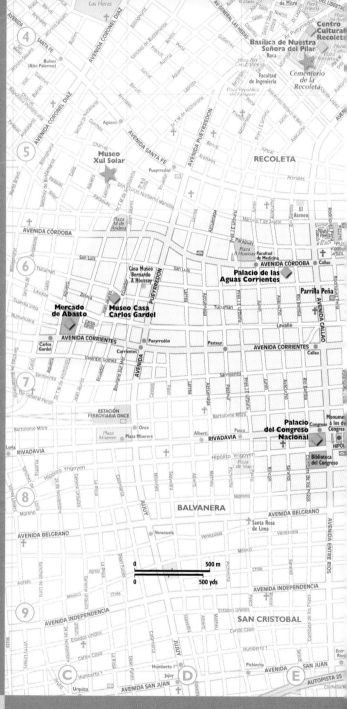

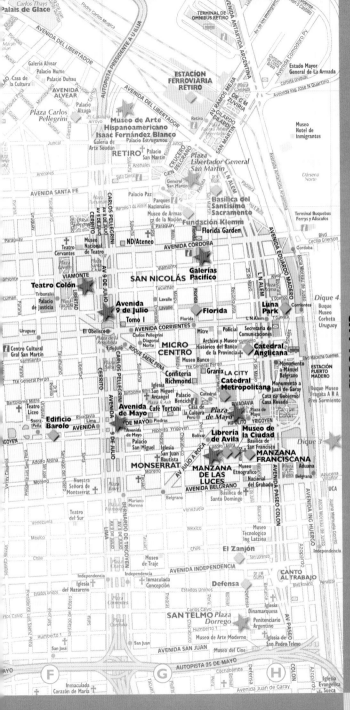

City Centre Quick Reference Guide

CITY TOURS

Avenida 9 de Julio (▷ 14)

A mammoth street where the giant, landmark El Obelisco towers over the traffic; its excessive scale epitomizes the city's grandeur.

Avenida de Mayo (▷ 16)

Lined with handsome buildings, this grand avenue links the parliament to the presidential palace. Along the way are some of the city's great cafés.

Galerías Pacífico (▷ 30)

A variety of shops, some showcases of high culture plus a mouth-watering food patio, under a vault of intriguing frescoes by leading Argentine artists.

Manzana de las Luces (▷ 34)

Under this rare remnant of the city's colonial past, including former seats of power, lurks an 18th-century warren of tunnels once used by smugglers.

Plaza de Mayo (▷ 54)

A neoclassical cathedral, the colonial city hall and the attractive, rose-hued presidential palace—three major sights loom over the city's main square.

Teatro Colón (▷ 60)

Restored to its former glory just in time for the 2010 Bicentenary, Buenos Aires' opera house is truly world-class, with superb acoustics attracting international performers.

Boca and San Telmo

The earthy southern *barrios* are edgy and vibrant: gutsy little Boca with its multicoloured houses and chocolate-box football stadium; and decadent San Telmo, where tango and antiques make a perfect marriage—this is where the city was first founded.

Morning
Take a taxi to **La Bombonera** (▷ 18–19) soccer stadium and museum in Boca—the first tours begin around 10am (you might get tickets for a match, too). Then walk straight to the Riachuelo—you might like to choose between more conventional art by Quinquela Martín in the **Museo de Bellas Artes de la Boca** (▷ 73) or cutting-edge contemporary works in the impeccably renovated **Fundación PROA** (▷ 70).

Mid-morning
A late-morning stroll along the city's most photographed street, **El Caminito** (▷ 22–23), will help you work up an appetite. You could have a coffee, buy some trinkets or just watch the street tango displays, but do not be tempted to stray too far, as pickpockets and worse await their victims in the tough streets of Boca.

If it is a weekday, you might like to speed to San Telmo (by taxi) and take a pre-prandial tour of the **Pasaje San Lorenzo** and **El Zanjón** (▷ 75; right). If it is Sunday you should try to squeeze in this trip down memory lane in the afternoon.

Lunch
Good eating is limited in Boca, though some hearty pasta might tempt you to hang around—try **Il Matterello** (Martín Rodríguez 517; tel 4307-0529; closed Mon), but get a taxi there. San Telmo has a far wider choice, though. **La Brigada** (▷ 143–144) is a great place for simple meat while **Orígen** (▷ 148) is an honest vegetarian option.

Afternoon
On weekends, especially Sundays, the place to head for in San Telmo is **Plaza Dorrego** (▷ 52–53). All manner of antiques, crafts and artworks draw in the crowds, as does the alfresco tango spectacle, weather permitting. Go Monday to Friday and you'll have to make do with the Montmartre-like charm (without the crowds) of a small artsy plaza. **Calle Defensa** (▷ 66), however, is lined with fabulous antiques shops and art galleries.

Mid-afternoon
Wind up a fascinating afternoon in bohemian San Telmo with a visit to the area's leading museum, the **Museo Histórico Nacional** (▷ 42–43), which is conveniently located in the neighbourhood's finest park, the equally historic **Parque Lezama** (▷ 50–51; left). The latter comes into its own in the late afternoon, when mellow light falls on the palms and shrubs.

Evening
This is tango country —choose between a memorable concert at the **Centro Cultural Torquato Tasso** (▷ 134) and a classic show at **El Querandí** (▷ 137; right).

Dinner
Adventurous diners will head for **La Vinería de Gualterio Bolívar** (▷ 151) for minimalist cuisine; otherwise there are plenty of simpler options, such as **Lezama** (Brasil 359; tel 4361-0114).

AVENIDA BELGRANO

(8)

AVENIDA ENTRE RIOS

Teatro
del Sur

Mariano
Moreno

Belgrano

Venezuela

Venezue

Plaza
Formosa

BERNARDO DE YRIGOYEN

AV 9 DE JULIO

LIMA

AV 9 DE JULIO

Mexico

Combate de los Pozos

Virrey Cavallos

Solís

Chile

Tacuari

Museo
de Traje

AVENID

Plaza
Chaco

AVENIDA INDEPENDENCIA

Independencia

Independencia

Inmaculada
Concepción

(9)

Carlos Calvo

Presidente Luis Sáenz Peña

San José

Santiago del Estero

Estados Unidos

Iglesia
del Nazareno

Piedras

Salta

Plaza
Corrientes

SANT

Plaza
Córdoba

Chacabuco

Humberto 1

Humberto 1

Entre
Ríos

San José

San Juan

AVENIDA SAN JUAN

AVENIDA SAN JUAN

AUTOPISTA 25 DE MAYO

AUTOPIST

Cochabamba

Santa
Teresa

Cochabamba

Cochabamba

Inmaculada
Corazón de María

Piedras

Solís

Constitución

CONSTITUCIÓN

LIMA

Tacuari

(10)

Sarandí

AVENIDA ENTRE

Filiberto

Pavon

Plaza
de la
Constitución

Avenid

Plaza Garay

Av Juan de Garay

Combate de los Pozos

Ciudadela

AV BRASIL

Tacuari

Foro
Judicial

RIOS

Antequera

Momboe

Presidente Luis Sáenz Peña

Virrey Cavallos

Avenida Brasil

San José

Santiago del Estero

Salta

O'Brien

Constitución

LIMA

PLAZA
CONSTITUCIÓN

Dr E
Finochieto

Pedro Echague

Solís

Pedro
Echague

15 de Noviembre de 1889

General Hornos

15 de Noviembre
de 1889

Rondeau

Plaza
España

Dr E Finochietto

Paracas

Dr E Finochietto

Ituzaingo

AVENIDA 9 DE JULIO

(11)

AVENIDA CASEROS

Jardín
Botánico
del Sur

Ambrosio
Olmos

Quinquela

Herrera

Juan C Gómez

AVENIDA VELEZ SARSFIELD

Dr E Finochietto

Balcarce

Uspallata

Pedriel

Anchoris

AVENIDA AMANCIO ALCORTA

Santa
Cruz

Uspallata

Lizuriaga

Los Patos

Ciudad de
Sóggdel

Dr R Carrillo

Aristóbulo
del Valle

Salmun Feijoo

Oncativo

Brandsen

(12)

AV AMANCIO ALCORTA

José A Cortejarena

Lanin

Icalma

Aceralmi

Cochue

Criel Rico

Suárez

General Hornos

Mirave

Mirave

Beaunn

BARRACAS

Suárez

Olavarria

Herrera

0   500 m
0   500 yds

E

F

G

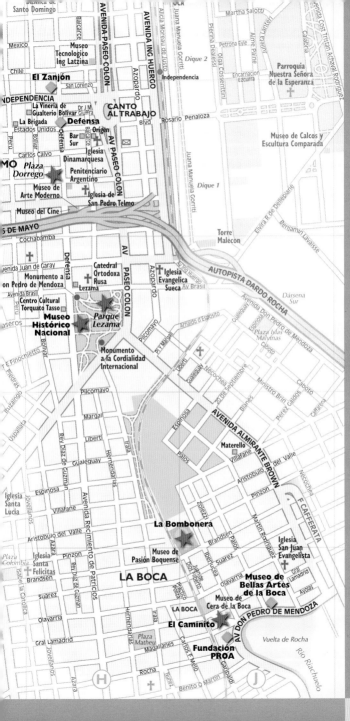

Boca and San Telmo Quick Reference Guide

TOP 25 SIGHTS AND EXPERIENCES

La Bombonera—Boca Juniors Stadium (▷ 18)

Small but beautifully formed, the Boca Juniors' stadium, the city's best known temple to soccer, is nicknamed the Chocolate Box due to its diminutive size.

El Caminito (▷ 22)

See brightly painted houses and impromptu dancing along the Boca street named after a famous tango—postcard manufacturers love it. Visitors can buy works by local artists.

Museo Histórico Nacional (▷ 42)

Get the lowdown on the country's turbulent past through paintings and other rich collections in this Italianate wedding cake building—a must for all history buffs.

Parque Lezama (▷ 50)

This delightful San Telmo park, donated to the city by the widow of landowner José Gregorio Lezama, marks the spot where Buenos Aires was first founded back in 1536

Plaza Dorrego (▷ 52)

Come to this San Telmo square for the Sunday Feria de San Telmo with an eye for a bargain and an ear for tango—and a hand firmly on your belongings. On other days enjoy the architecture.

Retiro and Recoleta

In this brace of classy northern neighbourhoods three of Buenos Aires' finest art museums vie for attention with the world's most elegant cemetery, alongside a couple of beautiful churches, a plaza surrounded by palaces and a giant metal flower.

Morning
La Biela (▷ 143) is one of the city's best-known *confiterías* and just the place to start the day in Buenos Aires' classy northern *barrios*. You can then cross the road and see Evita's grave in the melancholy but beautiful **La Recoleta cemetery** (▷ 24–25) before the crowds arrive. If you feel up to some meditation, peek inside the stunning **Basílica de Nuestra Señora del Pilar** (▷ 66; right).

Mid-morning
If you are feeling energetic you could stroll as far as the *Floralis Genérica* (▷ 69), one of the city's newest landmarks. Shopaholics will enjoy the wide range of shops in **Patio Bullrich** (▷ 126), where you could also have a coffee or even linger for an early lunch.

Alternatively, move across to Retiro (take a taxi), where the delights of leafy **Plaza San Martín** (▷ 56–57) await. Before lunch it might be possible to fit in the remarkable **Basílica del Santísimo Sacramento** (▷ 66), the Sacré-Coeur's doppelganger. Or investigate the great art collection in the **Fundación Klemm** (▷ 69). Two examples of Anglo-Argentine architecture nearby are the **Estación Retiro** (▷ 68), with its Royal Doulton tiles, plus the Torre de los Ingleses, a clock-tower that vaguely resembles the one housing Big Ben in London.

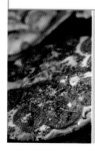

Lunch
Plaza San Martín is a wonderful place for a picnic but if you'd rather sit at a proper table try **Tancat** (▷ 150) for Spanish-style seafood, or **Filo** (▷ 146) for a great pizza. Those of you who indulge in retail therapy at Patio Bullrich might like the menu at **Francesca** (tel 4814-7513).

Afternoon
Winding along Calle Arroyo, with its art galleries, is a premium route to the fine **Museo de Arte Hispanoamericano Isaac Fernández Clanco** (▷ 36–37; left). Rest a while in the garden; there is more high culture to come.

Mid-afternoon
Two more art museums might give you indigestion, so it is either a panorama of European and Argentine painting and sculpture at the **Museo Nacional de Bellas Artes** (▷ 46–47) or a cameo of idiosyncratic works at the **Museo Xul Solar** (▷ 48–49).

Evening
This has been a gruelling programme so either sip champagne at **Milión** (▷ 136; right) or sup a pint at the **Shamrock** (▷ 133). Should you get your second wind, Recoleta hosts some of the wildest clubs among its genteel mansions—not least gay **Contramano** (▷ 135).

Dinner
Recoleta is all about elegance so you should put on the glad rags and sample refined gastronomy at **Oviedo** (▷ 148) or push the boat out even further and relish Gallic cuisine at **La Bourgogne** (▷ 143). If you don't mind noise and rough-and-ready service, indulge in a pizza at **El Cuartito** (▷ 145).

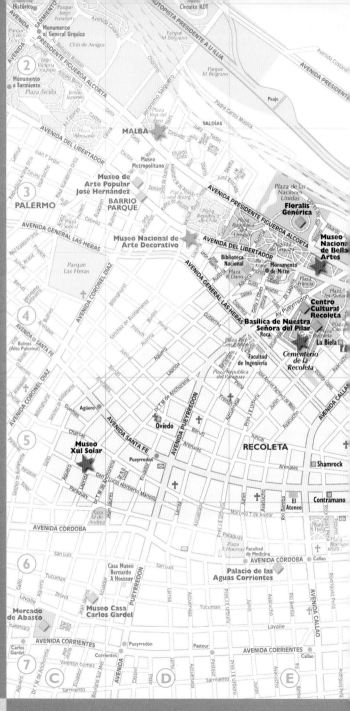

Río de la Plata

0   500 m
0   500 yds

Dársena F
Dársena E
Dársena D
Dársena C

RAMON S CASTILLO

NUEVO
PUERTO

Gendarmeria
Nacional

AUTOPISTA PRESIDENTE A U ILLIA

na Gral Juan Facundo Quiroga

Padre Carlos Mugica

Av Presidente Ramon

Comodoro Pedro I Zanni

Parque
Carlos Thays

Palais de Glace

AVENIDA DEL LIBERTADOR

TERMINAL DE
OMNIBUS RETIRO

Av de los Immigrantes

Comodoro Py

Estado
Mayor
General de
La Armada

La
ourgogne

Galería
Alvear

Patio Bullrich
Francesca

Palacio Hume
Palacio Duhau

Casa de
la Cultura

AVENIDA
ALVEAR

Palacio
Alzaga

ESTACIÓN
FERROVIARIA
RETIRO

AV RAMOS MEJIA
AV C ILARDO

Plaza Carlos
Pellegrini

Museo de Arte
Hispanoamericano
Isaac Fernández Blanco
Galería de
Arte Soudan

Palacio Estrugamou

Retiro

AV C ILARDO

Museo
Hotel de
Inmigrantes

RETIRO

Torre de los
Ingleses

Palacio
San Martín

Plaza
Libertador
General
San Martín

Dársena
Norte

AVENIDA SANTA FE

El Cuartito

Palacio Paz

Parques
Nacionales
Museo de Armasde la Nación
Tancat

General
San Martín

Basílica del
Santísimo
Sacramento
Filo
Fundación
Klemm

Terminal
Buquebus
Ferrys y
Aliscafos

Teatro
Cervantes

Museo
Nacional
de Teatro

AVENIDA CÓRDOBA

Córdoba

Galerías
Pacifico

Viamonte

AVENIDA EDUARDO MADERO

Tribunales
Palacio
de justicia

VIAMONTE

Plaza
Lavalle

SAN NICOLÁS

Tucuman

Lavalle

Florida

Buque
Museo
Corbeta
Uruguay

Teatro
Colón

Avenida
9 de Julio

Lavalle

Florida

Florida

Luna
Park

AVENIDA CORRIENTES

Carlos
Pellegrini

Centro
Cultural
Gral San
Martin

El Obelisco

Diagonal
Norte

MICRO
CENTRO

Mitre

Policial
Secretaria de
Comunicaciones

Archivo y Museo
Histórico del Banco
de la Provincia

Museo Banco
Tte General Perón

Catedral
Anglicana

Monumento
a Manuel
Belgrano

Plaza de la
República
9 de Julio

LA CITY

ESTACIÓN
PUERTO
MADERO

F
G
H

SIGHTS AND EXPERIENCES

Cementerio de la Recoleta
(▷ 24)
Among the monumental grave-stones is Eva Perón's modest last resting place in her family tomb—some say it is a tribute to a civilization yet to emerge.

Museo de Arte
Hispanoamericano Isaac
Fernández Blanco (▷ 36)
Colonial silverware and paintings displayed alongside remarkable furniture and Spanish tiles, in a fabulous neocolonial mansion.

Museo Nacional de Bellas
Artes (▷ 46)
Upstairs for Argentine and pre-Columbian artwork and downstairs for the Old World masters who inspired it—a fascinating lesson in comparative art.

Museo Xul Solar (▷ 48)
Find out about the man who invented a dozen new religions after lunch and see his distinctive paintings—Xul Solar is a leading figure of Argentine national art and a fascinating polymath.

Plaza San Martín (▷ 56)
Picnic alongside office workers beneath a giant rubber tree in the heart of classy Retiro, under the watchful eye of the Great Liberator, whose great bronze statue is a focal point.

Palermo

Vast parks, lush gardens and a grandiose racecourse justify
Palermo's green credentials, while its reputation for urban
sophistication rests on its attractive architecture, trendy restaurants,
modish nightlife and dozens of boutiques, as well as boutique
hotels. There are some fabulous museums, too.

Morning

A stroll or gentle jog around the **Parque
Tres de Febrero** (▷ 20–21; left) is an
excellent way to start the day, but keep
to the main paths if you are alone. You
could focus on the Jardín Japonés for its
zen landscaping and have an invigorating
cup of green tea in the tea-house. Or
kick-start with an espresso at **Un'Altra
Volta** (▷ 151), better known for its ice
cream but serving delicious cakes and
tarts, too.

Mid-morning

The charming **Jardín Botánico Carlos Thays** (▷ 32–33) could be
your next stop, though you may want to take a good look at the
dazzling **Monumento de los Españoles** (▷ 72) en route. If you are
with children, they might prefer the **Jardín Zoológico** (▷ 70), right
next door.

Get to the **Museo de Arte Latinoamericano de Buenos Aires**
(▷ 38–39; below)—known to all, including taxi drivers (you should
hail a cab), as 'el MALBA'—at midday, when it opens its doors to the
public. This will give you a good hour to discover the incredible main
collection of Latin American art or seek out the temporary show, if
there is one, before lunch.

Lunch

The MALBA has an excellent café-restaurant,
with tables inside and out, so why look any
further? However, since your next stop is the
Museo Nacional de Arte Decorativo, housed
in a Parisian-style *palais*, you could also walk
there and lunch in style at **Croque Madame**,
the exquisite restaurant located in the
palace's gatehouse.

Afternoon

You might just make it to the **Museo Nacional de Arte Decorativo** (▷ 44–45; right) in time for a guided tour (2.30pm) of this sumptuous palace and its equally eye-popping contents; of course, you can also visit the museum at your own pace.

Mid-afternoon

Break up the afternoon in **Palermo Viejo**, specifically **Palermo Soho**, shopping (▷ 58–59) heaven. Both **b-Blue Deli and Natural Bar** (▷ 142) and **Mark's Deli** (▷ 147) offer much-needed breaks. Finish the afternoon in style with a visit to the **Museo Evita** (▷ 40–41)—the name speaks for itself.

Evening

Palermo's nightlife is as varied as the *barrio* is huge. **Antares** (Armenia 1447; tel 4833-9611) serves real ale from 7pm, while night owls might prefer **Congo** (▷ 135) for late-night cocktails. Jazz fans will love **Thelonious** (▷ 137) but if you are looking for a gaucho blockbuster, book a table at **Ópera Pampa** (▷ 76; left).

Dinner

Palermo's top-notch restaurants are so numerous it is hard to single any out, but **Don Julio** (▷ 145) is unbeatable for steak, the city's best Asian restaurant has to be **Sudestada** (▷ 150) and **Ølsen** (▷ 148) still stands out for sheer style.

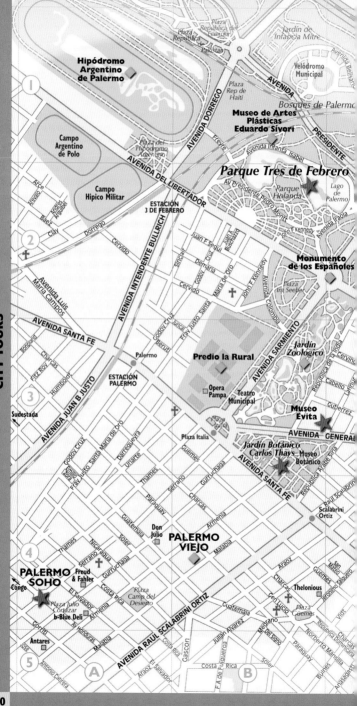

Plaza
República del
Perú

Jardín de
Infancia Mitre

Plaza
República
de Pakistán

Velódromo
Municipal

AVENIDA BELISARIO

**Hipódromo
Argentino
de Palermo**

AVENIDA

Plaza
Rep de Haití

1

Bosques de Palermo

**Museo de Artes
Plásticas
Eduardo Sívori**

AVENIDA DORREGO

Freire

Avenida Infanta Isabel

PRESIDENTE

**Campo
Argentino
de Polo**

Plaza del
Hipódromo
Argentino

AVENIDA DEL LIBERTADOR

Parque Tres de Febrero

Av Presidente Pedro Montt

**Parque
Holanda**

Lago
de
Palermo

Arce

Arévalo

Andrés Aguilar

Báez

Clay

Dorrego

Cervido

**Campo
Hípico Militar**

**ESTACIÓN
3 DE FEBRERO**

AVENIDA INTENDENTE BULLRICH

Juan F Segui

Julián Buschiazzo

Sinclair

John F Kennedy

Avenida Paola

**Monumento
de los Españoles**

2

Avenida Luis María Campos

Demaría

Godoy
Cruz

María de Oro

John F Kennedy

Avenida Colombia

Plaza
Int Seeber

Bompland

AVENIDA SANTA FE

Cervido

Cerviño

Juncal

Fray Justo Santa

República de la India

Cervido

Charcas

Fitz Roy

Humboldt

Palermo

Godoy Cruz

Cerrito

Predio la Rural

AVENIDA SARMIENTO

**Jardín
Zoológico**

Cabello

República de la India

Gutiérrez

3

**ESTACIÓN
PALERMO**

AVENIDA JUAN B JUSTO

Sudestada

Godoy Cruz

Fray Justo Santa María de Oro

Emilio

Pedro

Darregueyra

Uriarte

**Opera
Pampa**

**Teatro
Municipal**

**Museo
Evita**

AVENIDA GENERAL

Plaza Italia

AVENIDA SANTA FE

Thames

Serrano

Gurruchaga

Plaza Italia

**Jardín Botánico
Carlos Thays** Museo
Botánico

República Árabe Siria

Paraguay

Charcas

Raúl Scalabrini

Cuatemala

Armenia

Araoz

Scalabrini
Ortiz

4

Thames

Nicaragua

Soler

**Don
Julio**

Malabia

Araoz

Charcas

Guemes

San Mateo

**PALERMO
SOHO**

Congo

Serrano

**Freud
& Fahler**

Gurruchaga

Costa Rica

**PALERMO
VIEJO**

Central

Thelonious

Jerónimo Salguero

El Salvador

Plaza
Camp del
Desierto

Gurruchaga

Cuatemala

Central

Plaza
Guemes

República Dominicana

Charcas

Plaza Julio
Cortázar

b-Blue Deli

Armenia

Honduras

Malabia

AVENIDA RAUL SCALABRINI ORTIZ

Medrano

Norberto Mansilla

Antares

Gorriti

José

Antonio Cabrera

Julián Álvarez

Gascón

Costa Rica

Paraguay

Bulnes

Ambassador

5

F.A de Figueroa

Araoz

El Salvador

Costa Rica

Soler

A

B

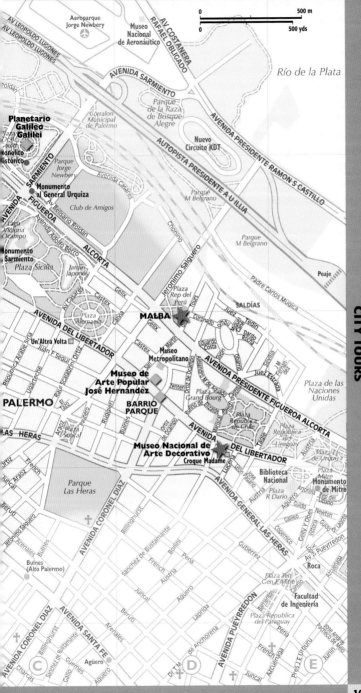

Aeroparque
Jorge Newbery

Museo
Nacional
de Aeronáutico

Río de la Plata

AV LEOPOLDO LUGONES
AV LEOPOLDO LUGONES

AVENIDA SARMIENTO

AV COSTANERA RAFAEL OBLIGADO

0   500 m
0   500 yds

Parque
de la Raza
Bosque
Alegre

AVENIDA PRESIDENTE RAMON S CASTILLO

**Planetario
Galileo
Galilei**

Plaza
Dr B
South
**Monolito
histórico**

SARMIENTO

Corralón
Municipal
de Palermo

Parque
Jorge
Newbery

Nuevo
Circuito KDT

AUTOPISTA PRESIDENTE A U ILLIA

**Monumento
al General Urquiza**

Av BELGRANO Roldan

Avenida Casares

AVENIDA

FIGUEROA

Plaza
Victoria
Ocampo

Avenida Adolfo Berro

Club de Amigos

Chopino

Parque
M Belgrano

ALCORTA

**Monumento
Sarmiento**

Plaza Sicilia

Jardín
Japonés

Av Casares

Parque
M Belgrano

Peaje

Jerónimo Salguero

Padre Carlos Mugica

Celix

Plaza
S Rep
del Perú

Castex

SALDÍAS

Plaza
Alemania

AVENIDA DEL LIBERTADOR

Celix

Castex

MALBA

Juez Tedin

Coronado

Juez
pardo
Rocha

Eduardo
Costa

Plaza de las
Naciones
Unidas

Un'Altra Volta

Juan F Segui Ortiz

Raul Scalabrini Ortiz

República Arabe Siria

Libertador

Arce

Uriarte

**Museo
Metropolitano**

Alfredo de Campo

Ombu

Juez Estrada

AVENIDA PRESIDENTE FIGUEROA ALCORTA

**Museo de
Arte Popular
José Hernández**

Zentener

Rufino de Elizalde

PALERMO

Ruggieri

Araoz

Plaza
Sobral

Ortiz
de Ocampo

Bulnes

**BARRIO
PARQUE**

Plaza
Grand Bourg

Plaza
República
de Chile

AVENIDA

DEL LIBERTADOR

Plaza
República
del Uruguay

Plaza V
de Urquiza

Marechal

Faxaje

Austria

LAS HERAS

Ortiz

French

Araoz

**Museo Nacional de
Arte Decorativo**
Croque Madame

Lucena

José Paino

AVENIDA GENERAL LAS HERAS

**Biblioteca
Nacional**

Plaza
R Darío

Austria

Plaza
Mitre

**Monumento
de Mitre**

Rep del
Libano

Juncal

Jerónimo Salguero

Arenales

Bulnes

Parque
Las Heras

AVENIDA CORONEL DIAZ

Billinghurst

Agüero

Sanchez de Bustamante

French

Austria

Pena

Bollini

Gutierrez

Galileo

Ceny Robes

Vittora

Newton

Av F Puyrredon

Cosmono

Dr J Laprida

Berutti

Bulnes
(Alto Palermo)

Juncal

Berutti

Arenales

Juncal

Pena

Labrida

Aguero

Plaza Ten
Gen E Mitre

Conino

Roca

Azcuenaga

**Facultad
de Ingeniería**

AVENIDA CORONEL DIAZ

AVENIDA
SANTA FE

Billinghurst

Sanchez de Bustamante

Charcas

Guemes

Gallo

Agüero

Berutti

Arenales

Dr M

de Anchorena

AVENIDA PUEYRREDON

Pena

Plaza
República
del Paraguay

Prest E Uriburu

Azcuenaga

Frenchena

Juncal

Jose Andres
Pacheco de Melo

Junin

Palermo Quick Reference Guide

Bosques de Palermo—Parque Tres de Febrero (▷ 20)
Duck ponds, rose gardens and a retro planetarium in Palermo's leafy fringe—a great place for a lazy afternoon.

Jardín Botánico Carlos Thays (▷ 32)
The city's botanical gardens are named for Carlos Thays, a prolific Frenchman who created most of the country's parks and gardens.

Museo de Arte Latinoamericano de Buenos Aires (MALBA) (▷ 38)
Contemporary architecture with great vision housing modern Latin American art at its best.

Museo Nacional de Arte Decorativo (▷ 44)
Versailles meets the Rockefeller Center—a lesson in pomp and splendour, plus works by El Greco, Fragonard and Manet.

Museo Evita (▷ 40)
Haute couture and noble architecture: Argentina's most famous woman, despite her many detractors, is commemorated in style.

Shopping in Palermo Soho (▷ 58)
Shoes and shirts, carpets and CDs, soap and stationery— bohemian Palermo's many boutiques have it all.

Puerto Madero

A great place to stroll, this elegant neighbourhood is a thrusting mix of tastefully regenerated docklands, smart steakhouses and avant-garde galleries, plus a nature reserve where birdsong fills the air and pampas grass runs riot.

Morning
I Fresh Market (▷ 147) is the perfect place to start this leisurely tour of the city's newest and most hedonistic *barrio*. Take time for freshly roasted coffee and a fortifying breakfast. The ecological reserve at the Costanera Sur (▷ 26–27) opens around breakfast time, so you can beat the crowds. First, you might like to buy some provisions at I Fresh Market for a mid-morning picnic.

Mid-morning
Now head for the **Reserva Ecológica Costanera Sur** (right), a wonderful nature reserve on the city's doorstep, where you can spot toads and turtles, lizards and butterflies, and more than 200 bird varieties. If ornithology is an interest of yours, you might like to contact Aves Argentinas (www.avesargentinas.org.ar). Otherwise just wander around the reserve at leisure—though do protect yourself against sunstroke, dehydration and mosquito bites.

Lunch
Places to eat in Puerto Madero tend to be very up-market but there are plenty of great places with terraces, so this might be the time to splash out. **Bice** (▷ 143) and **Sottovoce** (▷ 150) are two excellent choices if Italian fare is to your liking, while **Siga La Vaca** (▷ 150) serves Argentine food with emphasis on steak.

Afternoon
One of the undoubted highlights of Puerto Madero's tourist attractions is the fantastic new art collection, the **Collección de Arte Amalia Lacroze de Fortabat** (▷ 29). You could easily spend an hour or two looking at this treasure of Argentine and international paintings, including works by Turner, the Brueghels, Chagall and Dali.

Mid-afternoon

Tea at **Tea Connection** (Olga Cossettini 1545, Loft 3, tel 4312-7315) or coffee at **The Coffee Store** (Alicia Moreau de Justo 291, tel 4311-1142)—what names could be easier?—might be just the ticket after that immersion in stunning artworks amassed by one of the country's richest women. Interestingly all of the streets in the *barrio* are named for female personalities, while one of the major sights is the appropriately feminine Puente de la Mujer (Woman's Bridge), a work by Santiago Calatrava that curves across one of the docks.

One of the ships permanently moored along Dique 4 is named after President Sarmiento and the enjoyable **Fragata *Presidente Sarmiento*** (▷ 28) is well worth a visit, as is the nearby **Corbeta *Uruguay*** (▷ 28), a Naval Academy vessel also moored here.

Evening

The tango show at the Faena Hotel+Universe's **Rojo Tango** (▷ 137) is a memorable affair, while trendy club **Asia de Cuba** (▷ 133) appeals to the poser in us all.

Dinner

Dinner at **Cabaña Las Lilas** (▷ 144; left) is a must if you are in the *barrio*, while dining at **El Bistro** in the Faena Hotel +Universe (▷ 143) is also an experience, if only for the decor.

5
6
7
8
9
E
F
G
Vicente López
Arenales
Libertad
Sgto Cabral
Libertador
General San Martín
Santa Fe
AVENIDA SANTA FE
El Ateneo
Rodríguez Peña
Montevideo
Paraná
Talcahuano
Plaza Tucumán
CARLOS PELLEGRINI
Palacio Paz
Marcelo T de Alvear
Parques Nacionales
Museo de Armas de la Nación
Fundación Klemm
Plaza Libertad
CERRITO
AV 9 DE JULIO
Plaza R Peña
Pizzurno
Uruguay
Suipacha
Paraguay
Esmeralda
Maipú
Plaza Rodríguez
Arturo
Teatro Cervantes
Museo Nacional de Teatro
AVENIDA CÓRDOBA
Callao
Plaza Lavalle
Plaza Santa Cruz
Viamonte
VIAMONTE
SAN NICOLÁS
Tucumán
Tribunales
LIBERTAD
Teatro Colón
Palacio de Justicia
Avenida 9 de Julio
Lavalle
AVENIDA CALLAO
Carlos Pellegrini
Río Bamba
El Obelisco
AVENIDA CORRIENTES
Plaza de la República
Diagonal Norte
MICRO CENTRO
Centro Cultural Gral San Martín
9 de Julio
Sarmiento
Plaza Salta
ROQUE SAENZ PEÑA
Tte General Perón
Dr B Rivarola
Iglesia San Miguel Arcangel
Bartolomé Mitre
Palacio Bencich
Plaza R Arlt
Teatro Liceo
AVENIDA
Avenida de Mayo
Congreso
Monumento a los dos Congresos
Sáenz-Peña
Palacio Barolo
Rivadavia
Lima
DE MAYO
Piedras
RIVADAVIA
Plaza del Congreso
Hipólito Yrigoyen
Chacabuco
Palacio del Congreso Nacional
HIPÓLITO YRIGOYEN
Palacio San Miguel
Iglesia San Juan Bautista
Biblioteca del Congreso
Presidente Luis Sáenz Peña
Santiago del Estero
Salta
9 DE JULIO
Adolfo Alsina
MONSERRAT
Combate de los Pozos
Solís
Virrey Cevallos
San José
Moreno
AV JULIO A ROCA
Nuestra Señora de Montserrat
Plaza Jujuy
Tacuarí
Belgrano
AVENIDA BELGRANO
Plaza Formosa
Mariano Moreno
Teatro del Sur
Venezuela
AVENIDA ENTRE RÍOS
BERNARDO DE IRIGOYEN
LIMA
Mexico
Chile
Plaza Chaco
Museo de Traje
AVENIDA INDEPENDENCIA
Independencia
Iglesia del Nazareno
Inmaculada Concepción
Estados Unidos
Plaza Corrientes
Carlos Calvo
SAN T
0
500 m
500 yds
Plaza Córdoba
Humberto 1
San José
San Juan
Sarandí
Entre Ríos
AVENIDA SAN JUAN
AUTOPISTA 25 DE MAYO
Santa Teresa

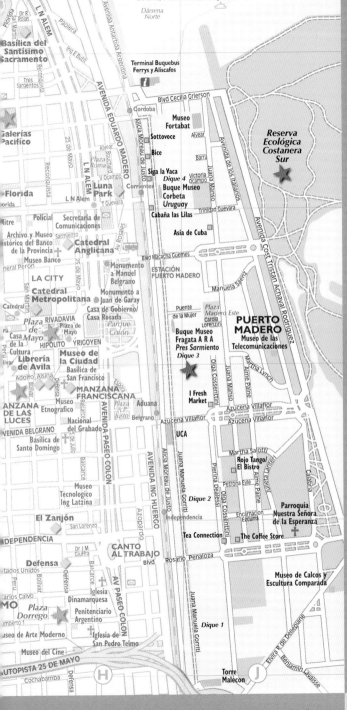

Colonia, Montevideo, Y Mapels

Dársena Norte

Florida

Dr R Rojas

Basílica del Santísimo Sacramento

AVENIDA ANTÁRTIDA ARGENTINA

Ing E Butt

Paolera

Galerías Pacifico

25 de Mayo

Alvear

Reconquista

L N ALEM

Plaza Roma

V Ocampo

Florida

L N Alem

T Guevara

Luna Park

AVENIDA EDUARDO MADERO

Alicia Moreau de Justo

Corrientes

Córdoba

Terminal Buquebus Ferrys y Aliscafos

Blvd Cecilia Grierson

Museo Fortabat

Alvear

Sottovoce

Bice

Barra

Siga la Vaca

Dique 4

Victoria Ocampo

Buque Museo Corbeta Uruguay

Cabaña las Lilas

Trinidad Guevara

AVENIDA de los Italianos

Juana Manso

Reserva Ecológica Costanera Sur

AVENIDA Cost Tristán Achával Rodríguez

Asia de Cuba

Mitre

Policial

Secretaría de Comunicaciones

Sarmiento

Archivo y Museo Histórico del Banco de la Provincia

Museo Banco

neral Perón

LA CITY

Catedral Anglicana

Blvd Macacha Güemes

ESTACIÓN PUERTO MADERO

Manuela Sáenz

Monumento a Manuel Belgrano

Catedral Metropolitana

Catedral

25 de Mayo

Perú

Plaza de Mayo

RIVADAVIA

Monumento a Juan de Garay

Casa de Gobierno/ Casa Rosada

Parque Colón

Puente de la Mujer

Plaza Madero Este

Plaza Carola Lorenzini

PUERTO MADERO

AVENIDA Cost Tristán Achával Rodríguez

Casa de la Cultura

HIPÓLITO YRIGOYEN

Plaza de Mayo

Buque Museo Fragata A R A Pres Sarmiento

Dique 3

Museo de las Telecomunicaciones

Olga Cossentín

Juana Manso

Martha Lynch

Librería de Avila

Adolfo Alsina

Museo de la Ciudad

Basílica de San Francisco

MANZANA FRANCISCANA

I Fresh Market

Aimé Painé

Bolívar

Museo Etnográfico

Plaza A P Justo

Aduana

Belgrano

Azucena Villaflor

Azucena Villaflor

ANZANA DE LAS LUCES

AVENIDA PASEO COLÓN

Nacional del Grabado

UCA

Azucena Villaflor

VENIDA BELGRANO

Basílica de Santo Domingo

Av 9 de Julio

Balcarce

Alicia Moreau de Justo

Juana Manuela Corriti

Martha Salotti

Rojo Tango/ El Bistro

Olga Cossentín

Aimé Painé

Petrona Eyle

Calabria

Museo Tecnológico Ing Latzina

Azopardo

Plena Dealessi

El Zanjón

San Lorenzo

AVENIDA ING HUERGO

Dique 2

Encarnación Ezcurra

Parroquia Nuestra Señora de la Esperanzá

DEPENDENCIA

Dr J M Giuffra

CANTO AL TRABAJO

Blvd

Independencia

Tea Connection

The Coffee Store

Defensa

stados Unidos

Perú

Bolívar

Balcarce

Defensa

Rosario Penaloza

Juana Manuela Corriti

Museo de Calcos y Escultura Comparada

arlos Calvo

MO

Plaza Dorrego

Umberto 1

Iglesia Dinamarquesa

Penitenciario Argentino

Dique 1

useo de Arte Moderno

Iglesia de San Pedro Telmo

Museo del Cine

AUTOPISTA 25 DE MAYO

Cochabamba

Defensa

(H)

Torre Malecón

(J)

Elvira F de Delepiane

Benjamín Lavaisse

Puerto Madero Quick Reference Guide

SIGHTS AND EXPERIENCES

Costanera Sur (▷ 26)
Black-necked swans and herons
lap it up in this nature reserve with
pampas and lagoons right on the
city's doorstep—locals and visitors
share their enthusiasm. Joggers
and bicyclists flock here and
walkers can take guided tours.

**Los Diques de Puerto Madero
(▷ 28)**
Gentrified docklands where trade
has given way to luxury. The fine
gallery here has outstanding
artworks and there is gourmet
dining and luxury lodgings. Historic
vesssels are moored here.

SHOP	**116**

Food and Drink   Winery
I Central Market

ENTERTAINMENT	**128**

Dance Clubs and Discos   Rojo Tango
Asia de Cuba
Tango Venues and *Milongas*

EAT	**138**

Cafés, Delis and Snacks   ***Parrillas***
I Fresh Market   Siga La Vaca
Fine Dining   **Vegetarian, Pasta and Pizza**
Ayres de Patagonia   Bice
El Bistro   Sottovoce
Cabaña Las Lilas
Chila

Further Afield

Immediately north of Palermo, Belgrano is an even leafier residential *barrio* where you can find one of the city's finest collections of Hispanic art. Further north still is one of the top destinations lying outside the city boundaries, El Tigre (▷ 62–63), perfect for idling away time on its many waterways. Within Buenos Aires proper are three more diverse attractions: a great cemetery in Chacarita, a natural science museum in Villa Crespo, and a weekend gaucho fair in remote Mataderos, in the city's far west.

JORGE NEWBERY
ARMADOR SR IGUAL
DEL
DEPORTE ARGENTINO
27 MAYO 1875
8 MARZO 1914

Morning
If you want to pack in a full day, grab a coffee and take the *subte* or a taxi to the **Cementerio de la Chacarita** (▷ 77; left). It is far less of a celeb than the fancy graveyard in Recoleta, but a magnificent sight nonetheless and the resting place of tango hero Carlos Gardel. If you are really on a whistle-stop tour, you may not be able to fit in a visit to the **Museo Argentino de Ciencias Naturales** (▷ 77), home to fascinating dinosaur remains, in Villa Crespo.

Mid-morning
Aim to be at the Retiro train station by mid-morning and have another coffee with a *medialuna* (kind of croissant; below) in the glorious **Café Retiro** (▷ 69) on the premises. Trains to Tigre are very regular so you shouldn't have long to wait.

Lunch
You should have time for a pleasant stroll along the waterways of this subtropical Venice before lunch. One of the best places for a leisurely meal is **Il Novo Maria Luján del Tigre** (▷ 147), in the heart of this enticing suburb.

Afternoon

If you do nothing else in Tigre, at least try to take a short **boat ride** through the lush waterways. Launches leave the **Estación Fluvial** at regular intervals (▷ 63; left). Trying to see the other sights, like the Museo de Arte, is really a tall order, though.

Mid-afternoon

Catch the train back towards the city, but this time get off at Belgrano station and walk a few blocks to the **Museo de Arte Español** (▷ 77), a treasure trove of Spanish artefacts. You can relax in the beautiful gardens and have an ice cream across the road at Persicco.

Evening

If you want to finish this hectic day with a flourish of folk dance and gaucho antics, hop in a cab and ask for the **Feria de Mataderos** (▷ 77; right)—provided it is not during March (when it is closed). It functions on Sunday for most of the year but switches to Saturday from December to February. Check the website first in any case since it's a long way to go to be disappointed. A snack from a streetside grill will keep hunger at bay until dinner time.

Dinner

You are probably better off heading back to your local *barrio* for dinner—the day will have been exhausting and you might even take advantage of your hotel restaurant. Should you be looking for somewhere special for that last Buenos Aires supper, a **parrilla** makes sense for a final taste of Argentine steak. **Don Julio** (▷ 145) in Palermo, **Parrilla Peña** (▷ 148–149) in the city centre and **Cabaña Las Lilas** (▷ 144) in Puerto Madero are classic choices.

FLORIDA

Juan B Justo

M Padilla

VICENTE LÓPEZ

El Tigre
Il Novo María
Luján del Tigre

Rivadavia

AV GENERAL PAZ

AV DEL LIBERTADOR

AV LEOPOLD

Parque Saavedra

Luis M Saavedra

Nuñez

NUÑEZ

AV CABILDO

GENERAL
SAN MARTÍN

Ejército Argentina

Parque Presidente Sarmiento

SAAVEDRA

COGHLAN

Belgrano C

**Museo de
Arte Español**

Persicco

San Martín

VILLA
URQUIZA

Coghlan

Drago

Belgrano R

BELGRANO

Grl Urquiza

AV DE LOS INCAS

Colegiales

Miguelete

Pueyrredón

COLEGIALES

AV SAN MARTÍN

VILLA
PUEYRREDÓN

VILLA
ORTUZAR

Federico Lacroze

AV FOREST

AV GENERAL PAZ

AGRONOMIA

Artigas

CHACARIT

Francisco Beiró

AV F BEIRÓ

Arata

**Cementerio
de la Chacarita**

AV SAN MARTÍN

La Paternal

Chacarita

F Moreno

Lynch

Devoto

El Libertador

PATERNAL

AV SAN MARTÍN

AV SAN MARTÍN

Devoto

VILLA
DEL
PARQUE

Villa del Parque

Saenz Peña

VILLA
DEVOTO

VILLA GRL
MITRE

AV M T DE ALVEAR

MONTE
CASTRO

VILLA
SANTA
RITA

AV J B JUSTO

AV GAONA

CABALLITO

Caballito

VILLA
REAL

VÉLEZ
SARSFIELD

VERSAILLES

VILLA
LURO

FLORES

Flores

AV J B JUSTO

FLORESTA

Floresta

AV JUAN BAUTISTA ALBERDI

AV DIRECTORIO

Ciudadela

Liniers

Villa Luro

AUTOPISTA

AUTOPISTA 25 D

AV RIVADAVIA

AV RIVADAVIA

AV GENERAL PAZ

LINIERS

Parque
Presidente
Nicolás
Avellaneda

AUTOPISTA PERITO MORENO (AU 9)

Cementerio

VILLA
SOLDAT

PARQUE
AVELLANEDA

AUTOPISTA PRES H CÁMPORA

MATADEROS

Feria de Mataderos

AV JUAN BAUTISTA ALBERDI

Parque Alte
Guillermo
Brown

Villa
Soldati

Pres Illia

AUTOPISTA TTE GRL LUIS J DELLEPIANE

AUTOPISTA PRES H CÁMPORA (AU 7)

VILLA
LUGANO

Villa Lugano

AV CNEL ROCA

Lago
Laguna

AV GENERAL PAZ

LA MANTANZA

Villa Madero

VILLA
RIACHUELO

Lago de
Regatas

Aeropuerto
Int de Ezeiza
"Ministro Pistarini"

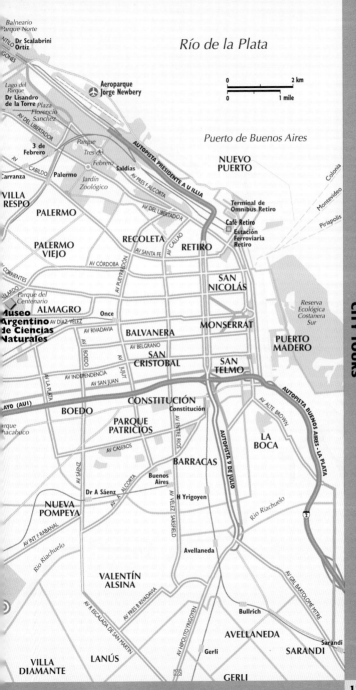

Río de la Plata

Puerto de Buenos Aires

Further Afield Quick Reference Guide

El Tigre (▷ 62)
A maze of waterways threads its way through a subtropical patchwork of languid islands. The main attractions are a range of water sports, and the Parque de la Costa theme park. A former casino houses an art gallery.

Shop

**Whether you're looking for the best
local products, a department store or a
quirky boutique, you'll find them all in
Buenos Aires. In this section shops are
listed alphabetically.**

SHOP

Introduction

Porteños love to shop, whether it is roving around smart malls choosing between international clothing brands and well-known local labels, hunting for bargains at antiques markets, or browsing through books and CDs. Although inflation has pushed prices up, there still are plenty of excellent deals to be had, and the quality of many goods is very high. Leatherware is especially good, while tango gear is worth checking out. If you are looking for a gift, maybe think local wines or traditional handicrafts.

Boutique *Barrio*

Like so many of the city's attractions, the bulk of the retail therapy opportunities are to be found in Palermo; above all, in Palermo Soho, where you can check out the latest fashions for women, men and kids. Designer goods galore jostle for space with original crafts to suit every budget—unusual stationery, novelty soaps and paraphernalia for drinking *mate*, the local tea-like brew, will make perfect gifts. That said, increasingly boho San Telmo and ever-chic Recoleta also have their fair share of specialist shops, selling everything from ornate waistcoats to handmade tango shoes.

WINE

Argentine wine has improved significantly since the 1990s. The region around Mendoza in the centre-west of the country produces some world-class wines these days, and the Malbec grape variety is the national flagship. You can also find some outstanding whites and sparkling wines along with other reds, such as Cabernet Sauvignon and Syrah. The vineyards in the northwest of the country, especially Cafayate, and northern Patagonia, near Neuquén, are up-and-coming regions to watch. Having sampled Argentine wine at some of the city's finest restaurants you might well want to take a bottle or two home.

Clockwise from top: Alto Palermo shopping mall; colourful Papelera Palermo; a record shop is a good place to find classic tango music; stalls in Plaza

Classy Malls

Porteños are justly proud of the city's shopping malls and galleries, many of which are listed buildings. A converted livestock market (Patio Bullrich, ▷ 126) and a former art deco food market (Mercado de Abasto, ▷ 172) are just two of the former, while the Galerías Güemes (▷ 124) is a downtown gem well worth visiting for its fine cupolas and handsome statuary.

Irresistible Bargains

You might do a double take when you look at the price label on many goods, though as everywhere you get what you pay for. Prices have soared, but they started at rock bottom, so there are still plenty of bargains, especially during sales (*liquidación*). Paying cash can get you an extra discount, and ask about tax refunds (IVA or VAT is currently 21 per cent).

Art and Antiques

San Telmo is dotted with antiques shops and small art galleries while the Sunday market on Plaza Dorrego (▷ 52–53) is popular; old soda siphons and tango collectables are favourite buys. Contemporary art is displayed at a number of exclusive galleries elsewhere—Argentine creativity seems to know no bounds.

SHOP

LEATHER

The world-famous cattle that graze the green, green grass of the pampa yield top-class hides as well as mouth-watering beef. No longer bargain-basement in terms of price, Argentine leather remains excellent value for money all the same. Shoes and slippers, attaché cases and handbags, wallets and belts, are just some of the fabulous items fashioned from calfskin, while jackets and coats to suit every taste are also on offer. Capybara leather (from a giant rodent native to northern Argentina)—known locally as *carpincho*—is highly regarded for its soft light-brown leather with an attractive mottled texture.

Serrano; Sabater Hermanos soap shop; Vellas de la Ballena candle shop

Directory

City Centre

Fashion
Etiqueta Negra
Leather Goods
Casa López
Malls
Galería Güemes
Galerías Pacífico
Tango Shopping
Bailarín Porteño
Quiosco del Tango
Zival's

San Telmo

Books and Records
Walrus Books
Crafts and Souvenirs
Decastelli
Tienda Diversa
Fashion
Balthazar
Leather Goods
En La Escalera
Tango Shopping
Gil Antigüedades

Retiro and Recoleta

Books and Records
Alberto Casares
Ateneo Grand Splendid
Notorious
Crafts and Souvenirs
Arandú
Buenos Aires Design
Fashion
Cora Groppo
La Dolfina
Leather Goods
Rossi & Caruso
Malls
Patio Bullrich
Tango Shopping
Comme Il Faut

Palermo

Accessories and Jewellery
Chicco Ruiz
Humawaca
Infinit
Manu Lizarralde
Sabater Hermanos
Books and Records
Miles
Crafts and Souvenirs
Arte Étnico Argentino
Papelera Palermo
Fashion
Balthazar
El Cid
Juana de Arco
Mimo & Co
Pesqueira
Food and Drink
Lo de Joaquín Alberdi
Leather Goods
Calma Chicha
Malls
Alto Palermo

Puerto Madero

Food and Drink
I Central Market
Winery

SHOP

Shopping A–Z

ALBERTO CASARES

www.acasares.servisur.com

Outstanding bookshop specializing in old, rare and out-of-print editions plus a splendid array of maps and prints, all sold with style in this venerable family establishment all done out in gleaming wood.

➕ G6 ✉ Suipacha 251 ☎ 4322-6198 ⏰ Mon–Fri 10–2, 3–8, Sat 10–2 🚌 9 de Julio

ALTO PALERMO

www.altopalermo.com.ar

Strategically located in Alto Palermo—Palermo Heights—this large shiny mall positively bursts with tempting shops, including reliable Argentine off-the-peg chains. You will also find a branch of Yenny's, the nationwide bookshop chain, where you can find some excellent coffee-table editions to take home or try your hand at Argentine literature.

➕ C4 ✉ Santa Fe 3253 ☎ 5777-8000 ⏰ Daily 10–10 🚇 Estación Buines (D)

ARANDÚ

www.arandu.com.ar

This shop in Retiro (with a Recoleta branch) is a perfect example of a great Argentine institution, the *talabartería*. They will fit you out in gaucho style, with traditional belts, stylish hats, gaudy espadrilles and all manner of shirts. *Mate* paraphernalia and beautiful knives with bone or wooden handles are in stock.

➕ F6 ✉ Paraguay 1259/Ayacucho 1924 ☎ 4816-3689/4800-1575 ⏰ Mon–Fri 10–8.30, Sat 9.30–1.30 🚌 59, 111

ARTE ÉTNICO ARGENTINO

www.arteetnicoargentino.com

Stupendous home-woven rugs and other textiles from the northwest of Argentina, plus offbeat wooden furniture are the mainstay at this enticing store.

➕ A4 ✉ El Salvador 4656 ☎ 4832-0516 ⏰ Mon–Fri 11–7, Sat 11–3 🚌 34, 55, 161

ATENEO GRAND SPLENDID

The Grand Splendid was built as a theatre in 1919—Carlos Gardel (▷ 73) once sang on its stage. It was converted into a cinema a decade later but is now one of the world's most beautiful bookshops. There is a decent café at the back, but the real attraction, apart from the books, of course, is the magnificent interior, topped by a beautiful ceiling painted by Italian artist Nazareno Orlandi.

➕ E5 ✉ Avenida Santa Fe 1860 ☎ 4811-6104 ⏰ Sun–Thu 10–10, Fri–Sat 10am–midnight 🚇 Callao (D) 🚌 39, 152

BAILARÍN PORTEÑO

Should you want to kit yourself out from head to toe ready for that Buenos Aires' night at the *milonga* (tango event), this unassuming shop in San Nicolás is the place to come. Felt hats, sharp

---

ARTESANIA

Artesanía, or arts and crafts, gives employment to thousands of people across the country. Indigenous peoples such as the Wichí in the Chaco region eke a living out of basket weaving and their produce is often on sale in the capital. There are outdoor markets selling all manner of traditional goods around the city, including the one held in front of the Centro Cultural Recoleta and another staged at Boca's Caminito, while specialist shops offer high-quality carpets and other crafts, mainly from northwestern Argentina.

suits and swanky jackets for him, slinky dresses, giddily high heels and costume jewellery for her, plus books, CDs and DVDs about tango. What more do you need?

🔳 G7 ✉ Suipacha 251 ☎ No phone ◐ Mon–Fri 10–7, Sat 10–5 🚇 Diagonal Norte 🚌 Avenida de Mayo

BALTHAZAR
www.balthazarshop.com

This menswear store for the modern dandy has branches in San Telmo (and Palermo). Treat yourself or a friend to an alpaca wool scarf in fetching stripes or a silk tie with an offbeat design. The Italian-style shirts are made to match the elegant clubby blazers.

🔳 H9 ✉ Defensa 887/Gorriti 5131 ☎ 4300-6926 ◐ Mon–Sat 11–8 🚌 10, 29, 195 (San Telmo); 39, 55, 168 (Palermo)

BUENOS AIRES DESIGN
www.designrecoleta.com.ar

Several dozen Argentine design shops under one roof a stone's throw from Recoleta cemetery and the Pilar church. Most of the goods on sale are for the home, including wonderful items made of leather.

✉ E4 ✉ Pueyrredón and Libertador, Recoleta ☎ 5777-6000 ◐ Daily 10–9 🚌 10, 17, 60, 67, 92, 110

SHOPPING TOURS

Cicerones (www.cicerones.org.ar) and BA Local (www.balocal.com) are two excellent organizations offering, respectively, free tours by volunteers and paying tours led by professionals. Both include shopping tours in their programmes, often taking you to less well-known areas or stores, and even giving you a chance to get to know designers and other creators in the city.

CALMA CHICHA
www.calmachicha.com

This contemporary design shop sells great cowhide and leather rugs, handbags and beanbags.

🔳 A4 ✉ Honduras 4909, Palermo ☎ 4831-1818 ◐ Mon–Sat 10–8, Sun 2–8 🚌 39, 151, 168

CASA LÓPEZ
www.casalopez.com.ar

With a major branch in the Galerías Pacífico (and another in Patio Bullrich), this venerable house of leather has its headquarters on Plaza San Martín. Jackets and trenchcoats for both sexes come with matching bags, luggage, wallets and purses.

🔳 G6 ✉ Galerías Pacífico 241 ☎ 5555-5421 ◐ Daily 10–9 🚇 San Martín

CHICCO RUIZ
www.lourdeschiccoruiz.com.ar

The Imelda Marcos in you might get some satisfaction at this fabulous shoe shop in Palermo Soho. Lourdes Chicco Ruiz makes her footwear for fashion-conscious women in the old-fashioned way, using the finest leather.

🔳 A4 ✉ Thames 1780 ☎ 4831-1264 ◐ Mon–Sat 12–8 🚌 34, 55, 166

EL CID
www.elcid.us

El Cid is renowned for its superb tailoring and clean-cut menswear by Porteño designer Néstor Goldberg. Whether your look tends towards the classic or you prefer casual kit, El Cid has something for you, along with an impressive line of stylish accessories, bags and shoes thrown in for good measure.

🔳 A4 ✉ Gurruchaga 1732 ☎ 4832-3339 ◐ Mon–Sat 11–8, Sun 3–7 🚌 34, 55, 166

COMME IL FAUT

www.commeilfaut.com.ar

One of many well-concealed secrets along the oh-so-French Rue des Artisans, this Recoleta shoe shop just off smart Calle Arenales prides itself on stocking the best tango footwear that money can buy.

✚ F5 ✉ Arenales 1239, Rue des Artisans ☎ 4815-5690 🕙 Mon–Fri 11–7, Sat 11–3 🚌 39, 101, 111, 152

CORA GROPPO

www.coragroppo.com

Cora Groppo is one of Argentina's best-loved fashion designers. She is known for her use of texture in fabrics while the colour scheme is on the toned-down side.

✚ F5 ✉ Uruguay 1296, Recoleta ☎ 4815-8516 🕙 Mon–Sat 11–8, Sun 3–8 🚌 15, 55, 151

DECASTELLI

www.decastelli.com.ar

Osvaldo Decastelli is an original artist who specializes in highly decorative sculptures made out of corrugated cardboard, which he sticks together and cuts out in simple but striking shapes, before painting them to bring them to life. Toy-like in appearance, they are serious works of art and are fast becoming collector's items.

✚ H8 ✉ Chile 354 ☎ 4307-7822 🕙 Mon–Sat 11–7 🚌 10, 22, 29

EN LA ESCALERA

This shop's name means 'On the stairs', which describes its unusual setting. Open only at the weekends, during weekdays the owner visits customers at home or in hotels. His range of leather clothing focuses on elegant design with

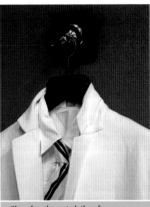

Shop for elegant clothes for men

the odd twist of contemporary flair.

✚ G8 ✉ Defensa 892, San Telmo ☎ 4855-0370 🕙 Sat–Sun 1–8 🚌 10, 22, 24, 29

LA DOLFINA

www.ladolfina.com

Polo heart-throb Adolfo Cambiaso has his own line of menswear that combines rural practicality with urbane chic. Ranging from well-cut bermuda shorts to best cotton dress shirts, and from polos and T-shirts to elegantly shaped jeans, the clothes here are smart casual at its very best.

✚ J8 ✉ Martha Salotti 454 ☎ 5787-5152 🕙 Mon–Fri 10–8, Sat 10–6 🚌 17, 59, 67, 102

ETIQUETA NEGRA

www.etiquetanegra.us

This classy menswear chain has branches in the Galerías Pacíficas (plus the Patio Bullrich and Unicenter shopping malls), as well as further afield in Las Cañitas and San Isidro. The slimfit suits, whiter-than-white cotton shirts and sleek leather shoes are expensive but they are made to last. There is a more limited women's range, too.

🚇 G6 ✉ Galerías Pacífico (▷ 30–31) ☎ 5555-5316 🕓 Daily 10–9 🚌 6, 93, 130, 152

GALERÍA GÜEMES

www.galeriaguemes.com.ar

Inaugurated in 1915, when it was considered the city's first sky-scraper, this historic building now has architectural heritage status, thanks to the gorgeous cupolas and palatial interior. Tikal chocolates and Vique polo- and golfwear, Blaquè leatherware for ladies and Boüzal menswear are just four of the great outlets here.

🚇 G7 ✉ Florida 165/San Martín 170 ☎ 4331-3041 🕓 Mon–Fri 8–8, Sat 9–3 🚇 Catedral

GIL ANTIGÜEDADES

www.gilantiguedades.com.ar

One of the leading antiques shops in San Telmo, Gil has been catering for locals and international clientele for decades and covers a wide gamut of artwork from the 18th century to the present day. Vintage clothing is one of its specialities.

🚇 H9 ✉ Humberto Primo 412 ☎ 4361-5019 🕓 Tue–Sat 11–1, 3–7, Sun 11–7 🚌 10, 22, 29, 126

HUMAWACA

www.humawaca.com

The ladies of Palermo and Recoleta (at Posadas 1380) like their handbags, so Humawaca has branches in both. The best Argentine leather is reborn as unusual clutches and purses, while two of the shop's exclusives are a shoulder bag with an iPod feature and a briefcase with a removable

solar panel that allows you to recharge appliances like mobile phones as you walk around.

🚇 A4 ✉ El Salvador 4692 ☎ 4832-2662 🕓 Mon–Sat 11–8, Sun 3–8 🚌 55, 151, 168

I CENTRAL MARKET

www.icentralmarket.com.ar

Twin to I Fresh Market (▷ 147), this enticing delicatessen has some of the best cakes and tarts in town, along with choice pasta, cheeses and cold cuts. The fresh fruits taste as good as they look. A great place to stock up for a picnic before venturing into the Reserva Ecológica.

🚇 J7 ✉ Pierina Dealessi and Macacha Güemes ☎ 5775-0330 🕓 Daily 8–midnight 🚌 2, 103, 152, 196

INFINIT

www.infinit.la

Glasses and sunglasses are very good value in Buenos Aires and what is more you can find some unique, fun designs here, so take your prescription with you. This alluring small shop in Palermo Soho specializes in retro frames, including a range decorated with sports cars. They will do their best to get them done within days.

🚇 A4 ✉ Thames 1602 ☎ 4831-7070 🕓 Mon–Sat 11–8, Sun 3–7 🚌 39, 55

JUANA DE ARCO

www.juanadearco.net

Mariana Cortés is the brain behind this fabulous Palermo boutique, with an art gallery down in the basement. Her multihued fabrics combine traditional South American techniques, such as Paraguayan lace, with contemporary designs, to create eye-catching garments and some very colourful underwear. She even turns her hand to some very avant-garde menswear, too.

🔲 A4 ✉ El Salvador 4762 ☎ 4833-1621
🕒 Mon–Sat 10–8, Sun 1–8 🚌 15, 34, 39

LO DE JOAQUÍN ALBERDI

www.lodejoaquinalberdi.com.ar

This outstanding Palermo *vinoteca* (wine store) puts on tastings of the amazing wines it sells. Otherwise just ask the extremely helpful staff for some guidance through the labyrinth of bottles that line the walls in this Aladdin's cave of reds, whites and sparklings from the country's leading bodegas, plus one or two off-the-beaten-track wineries, too.

🔲 A4 ✉ Jorge Luis Borges 1772 ☎ 4832-5329 🕒 Mon–Sat 11–9.30, Sun 12.30–9.30
🚌 34, 55, 93

MANU LIZARRALDE

www.manulizarralde.com

For rings and pendants, bracelets and necklaces, look no further than this Palermo gem where aquamarines, emeralds and amethysts are harmoniously combined with exotic stones by the master craftsman whose name the shop bears. The designs, such as the rutilated quartz earrings set in Argentine silver, are timelessly classical yet with a contemporary spark that really sets Manu's jewels apart.

🔲 A4 ✉ Gorriti 5078 ☎ 4832-6252
🕒 Mon–Sat 11–8, Sun 2–8 🚌 55, 151, 168

MILES

www.milesdiscos.com.ar

Sharing a landmark corner-house at the intersection with Gurruchaga with the marvellous Prometeo Libros bookshop, Miles (a tribute to jazz legend, Mr. Davis) is a

fertile hunting ground for jazz, tango and world music, plus genres less easy to find in Buenos Aires such as gospel, classical and international rock.

🔲 A4 ✉ Honduras 4912 ☎ 4832-0466
🕒 Mon–Thu 10–9, Fri–Sat 10–10, Sun 12–8
🚌 15, 39, 55, 140, 168

MIMO & CO

www.mimo.com.ar

This wonderful range of good-quality clothing and footwear for the under-12s is mostly on the smart side. The locals believe in spoiling their kids but at least they do it with style.

🔲 A4 ✉ El Salvador 4721 ☎ 4511-5180
🕒 Mon–Sat 11–8, Sun 2–8 🚌 15, 55, 168

NOTORIOUS

www.notorious.com.ar

This brilliant record shop where you can find all the latest in tango and jazz doubles up as a leading venue for live music. Jazz is particularly strong and you are bound to find something in their programming to please your eardrums.

🔲 E6 ✉ Avenida Callao 966 ☎ 4813-6888
🕒 Mon–Sat 10–8 🚇 Callao (D) 🚌 60, 86, 168

FACTORY OUTLETS

A square of prized real estate delineated by Avenidas Córdoba and Corrientes and Calles Julián Álvarez and Thames, Palermo Queen is of interest primarily for its mass of discount outlets. Paula Cahen d'Anvers (casual women's clothes), Lacoste, Grimoldi (smart casual for men, women and kids) and Prüne (handbags) all have stores here selling previous seasons' fashion, but most of their gear is timeless anyway. Prices are slashed by up to 70 per cent on the retail labels. For more on the city's outlets consult www.outlets-bsas.com.ar.

PAPELERA PALERMO

www.papelerapalermo.com.ar
Selling a fabulous array of home-made paper in a rainbow range of colours, this is a great place to pick up a photo album, a notepad or a diary, for those with old-fashioned stationery tastes.
✚ A4 ✉ Honduras 4945, Palermo
☎ 4833-3081 ◷ Mon–Sat 10–8, Sun 2–8
🚌 39, 55, 168

PATIO BULLRICH

www.shoppingbullrich.com.ar
Buenos Aires has no shortage of shopping malls that could make the most ardent mall-hater change their mind. This historic building used to be a livestock market, but its new lease of life as a glossy shopping centre is a great success. As at many local malls, the idea is to spend a whole afternoon checking out the latest fashion, people-watching at a café, sipping Bellinis at the bar and maybe segueing into an evening at the movies, or at a restaurant.
✚ F4 ✉ Posadas 1245 ☎ 4814-7400
◷ Daily 10–9 🚌 67, 92, 130

PESQUEIRA

www.pesqueiratm.com
Not far from Palermo's lively Plazoleta Cortázar hub, this delightful little boutique showcases designer Valeria Pesqueira's pretty women's clothes. Polka-dot prints and florals dominate the fresh, naive dresses and smocks, while the matching laptop bags are part of the apparel of all self-respecting Palermitanas. The prices are refreshing, too.
✚ A4 ✉ Armenia 1493 ☎ 4833-7218
◷ Mon–Sat 11–8 🚌 15, 55, 151, 168

QUIOSCO DEL TANGO

This tango kiosk is so much part of the city's culture it has been declared a national landmark. It dispenses all manner of items related to the national dance and music form, from books and magazines to sheet music and DVDs, plus a range of souvenirs that rival each other for tackiness.
✚ E7 ✉ Avenida Corrientes 1512
◷ Mon–Sat 9–7 🚇 Callao (D)

ROSSI & CARUSO

www.rossicaruso.com
Classy and classic leather goods for both sexes, from belts to handbags and briefcases to gloves, made using top-quality lizard and calfskin. Saddles, riding crops and tackle complete the range.
✚ F4 ✉ Posadas 1387, Recoleta ☎ 4811-1538 ◷ Mon–Fri 9.30–8, Sat 10–7 🚌 67, 92, 93

SABATER HERMANOS

www.shnos.com.ar
This Palermo landmark is run by the third generation of soap-makers—their shop is worth seeing even if you don't decide to take

the scented golf balls or marijuana-leaf soaps home with you as an ephemeral souvenir (though most of the designs look too good to wash with).

🔆 A4 ✉ Gurruchaga 1821 ☎ 4833-3004 🕐 Mon–Sat 10–8, Sun 1–7 🚌 83

TIENDA DIVERSIA

This excellent San Telmo shop sells a wide variety of unique pieces made by hand by dozens of artists, designers and craftspeople from different parts of the country. These include clothing, contemporary jewellery, handbags, decorative and functional items for the house, plus ethnic designs, artwork and an area for children.

🔆 H9 ✉ Humberto Primo 580 ☎ 4362-1262 🕐 Sun 11–2, 3–8 🚌 10, 22, 29, 126

WALRUS BOOKS

www.walrus-books.com.ar
Walrus, a real San Telmo landmark, is one of the best bookshops in the city if you are looking for anything in English. They stock more than 4,000 titles of old and new publications, covering a range of subjects from fiction to history.

🔆 H9 ✉ Estados Unidos 617 ☎ 4300-7135 🕐 Tue–Sun 12–8 🚇 Independencia 🚌 29, 130, 152

WINERY

www.winery.com.ar
Winery is a reliable chain of wine stores where you can find a comprehensive range of Argentine wines from every region.

🔆 J7 ✉ Avenida Juana Manso and Macacha Güemes ☎ 5290-6276 🕐 Mon–Sat 9–9, Sun 11–7 🚇 Plaza de Mayo 🚌 10, 17, 24, 29, 39

ZIVAL'S

www.zivals.com
If you are overwhelmed by the array of tango music on offer around the city, this is the place to come for some sound advice. The staff will talk you through the genres and artists and help you make that final choice of CD or DVD to take back home. It is also one of the city's best bookshops.

🔆 E7 ✉ Avenida Callao 395 🚇 Callao 🕐 Mon–Sat 9.30–10 🚇 Callao (B) 🚌 12, 24, 37, 60

Sabater Hermanos sells soaps in a range of traditional and fun shapes

Entertainment

Once you've done with sightseeing for the day, you'll find lots of other great things to do with your time in this chapter, even if all you want to do is relax with a drink. In this section establishments are listed alphabetically.

Introduction

Buenos Aires prides itself on its scintillating nightlife and quite rightly so. Locals party hard and late, with all-night festivities par for the course. When it comes to live music, obviously tango (▷ 6–7) tops the bill but jazz, rock and folk are all world-class, while opera and ballet, classic music and theatre complete the busy picture. The latter is mostly in Spanish but cabaret and musicals bring down any linguistic barriers.

Theatreland

Avenida Corrientes is Argentina's resounding answer to Broadway or the West End; it is lined with huge glitzy theatres staging the excellent home-grown versions of international musicals along with a glittering array of domestic drama and cutting-edge cabaret. The legendary Teatro Colón (▷ 60–61) is one of dozens of classical musical venues in a city where concerts are as numerous as steak suppers, and almost as good.

Bars and Pubs

It is unusual for Porteños to drink very much without eating, so wine bars and other drinking places usually serve food of some kind, even if only an assortment of tapas or a platter of cheese and cold cuts.

FREE FOR ALL

Going out to hear live music is seldom that pricey in Buenos Aires, with the main exceptions being gala tickets at the Colón or some of the more touristy venues like the Faena Hotel (▷ 156) or the tango shows aimed at foreigners. In the summer, you might even hear about free open-air concerts, held at various spots around the city. Watch for posters or flyers or ads in the press—El Obelisco has seen some fabulous concerts over the years, while the Palermo parks also host regular alfresco music fests as does the Parque Lezama (▷ 50–51).

Clockwise from top: Live music is a feature in many bars and clubs; the show at El Querandí; a poster show at Teatro Cervantes; Esqina Homero Manzi restaurant

Argentine champagne and classic cocktails are big favourites while increasing numbers of bars serve real ale, sometimes brewed on the premises. The lower riverside stretch of the city centre hosts many friendly bars and pubs. In other *barrios* people prefer to gather in *confiterías* to have more substantial meals with their glass of beer.

Fit and Healthy

Fitness and health are major obsessions in Buenos Aires. Gym membership rates are high, while sport tops every agenda. Taking part in all this exercise costs far less than in most major cities in the rest of the world. If relaxation is your thing you might like to be pampered in a spa—many hotels have their own. You will probably want an antidote to all that fabulous steak and wine.

Where to Go

Evening entertainment venues are scattered far and wide across the many *barrios* included in this guide. Most cinemas are housed in shopping malls, while concerts are held at football stadiums, purpose-built arenas, more intimate clubs or places that double up as restaurants or shops. Bars, pubs and nightclubs are focused in Palermo—noisy mega-discos gather along the riverside far from residential areas—but there are some in the city centre, Recoleta and even swish Puerto Madero.

ENTERTAINMENT

TICKETS

The best way to get tickets for most shows and events—sometimes at discounted prices—is to do so through one of the *carteleras*, or centralized box offices. Cartelera Baires is at Avenida Corrientes 1383 local 21, while Ticketek (www.ticketek.com.ar) has several outlets, including a central one at Viamonte 560, locales 6/8. Buy tickets online to save waiting in line.

---

has tango shows; the interior of Teatro Coliseo; a mural of tango singer Carlos Gardel (▷ 73)

Directory

ENTERTAINMENT

Entertainment A–Z

ALSINA

www.palacioalsina.com

This downtown clubbing venue has an impressive post-industrial decor and pulsates to the likes of John Digweed and M.A.N.D.Y. at the Saturday night 'State' and Friday night gay nights. Early birds can even get to bed by midnight if they attend the Sunday Club One, where a *thé dansant* starts at the civilized hour of 4pm.

G8 ⊠ Alsina 940 ☎ 4331-1277 ◎ Fri–Sat midnight–4, Sun 4–4 🚌 10, 17, 59, 64, 86 💷 $50 entry fee

ASIA DE CUBA

www.asiadecuba.com.ar

As you'd expect Puerto Madero's main dance club is a chic affair. Wednesdays see Glamour Nights when what you wear is more important than how you dance or the music played. People also visit for the good sushi and excellent drinks but you should expect to pay exorbitant prices.

J7 ⊠ Pierina Dialessi 750 ☎ 4894-1328 ◎ Mon–Wed 12.30–8pm, Thu–Sat 9pm–6am 🚌 2, 130, 152 💷 $70 entry fee

BAHREIN

www.bahreinba.com

One of the city's best downtown nocturnal venues, Bahrein features the Yellow Bar, an exclusive space for eating and drinking, while the Funky Room moves up a gear with dancing to mellow sounds under chandeliers. In XSS Excess leading DJs spin house music and trance.

G6 ⊠ Lavalle 345 ◎ Tue–Wed, Fri–Sat 12.30pm–6am 🚇 Leandro N. Alem 🚌 22, 28, 93, 152 💷 $50 entry fee

BAR SUR

www.bar-sur.com.ar

One of the most atmospheric San Telmo tango joints offers a memorable show. The corner-house and cobbled street have featured in films about tango's heyday.

H9 ⊠ Estados Unidos 299 ☎ 4362-6086 ◎ Daily 8pm–3am 🚌 29, 93, 130

BASEMENT CLUB–SHAMROCK

www.theshamrockbar.com

Like every city in the world, Buenos Aires has its Irish pubs but this doubles up as a popular dance club. It's busiest in the early hours.

The bar area at Asia de Cuba in Puerto Madero

Corrientes, or the dozen or so blocks either side of El Obelisco, is Buenos Aires' answer to Broadway or Leicester Square; it is home to theatreland. Much of the entertainment is in Spanish but there is plenty of cabaret, for example at the Teatro Belisario (No. 1624) or the Teatro Ópera (No. 860). The Teatro Gran Rex (No. 855) is a major venue for national and international music acts.

➕ E5 ✉ Rodriguez Pena 1220 ☎ 4812-3584 🕐 Thu–Sat 6pm–3am 🚌 39, 124, 152 💲 $10 (free for women)

BELUSHI MARTINI BAR

www.belushi.com.ar

Perfectly mixed negronis, margaritas and Martinis accompany appetizing two-serving *tablas*, snack boards covered with cheese, olives and other goodies, at this stylish cocktail bar in Palermo.
➕ A4 ✉ Honduras 5333 ☎ 4831-8665 🕐 Tue–Fri 12.30–6.30pm, Sat 2.30–8.30pm. Closed Sun–Mon 🚌 34, 55, 166

CAMPO ARGENTINO DE POLO

www.aapolo.com

The national polo pitch is in Palermo where the neighbouring mini-*barrio* of Las Cañitas is traditionally a hangout for polo players. It hosts the Argentine open championship every springtime.
➕ A1 ✉ Avenida del Libertador 4300 ☎ 4777-6444 🕐 Check schedule 🚌 15, 29, 55, 60 💲 $20–$200

CENTRO CULTURAL BORGES

www.ccborges.org.ar

In the Galerías Pacífico this arts centre puts on a wide range of photography and art shows as well as music and dance performances. Tango dominates but flamenco and folk get a look in.
➕ G6 ✉ Galerías Pacífico (Viamonte 525) ☎ 5555-5358 🕐 Box office: Mon–Sat 10–9, Sun noon–9 🚇 San Martín

CENTRO CULTURAL CARAS Y CARETAS

www.carasycaretas.org

This centre, run by a society magazine, mostly succeeds in presenting a broad array of art and culture. While plays in Spanish might have limited appeal, there are plenty of concerts and recitals, representing tango, jazz and folk. Interesting exhibitions of Argentine art are also held here.
➕ H8 ✉ Venezuela 370 ☎ 5354-6618 🕐 Check website 🚇 Florida

CENTRO CULTURAL TORQUATO TASSO

www.torquatotasso.com.ar

At this old-fashioned café-concert venue in the heart of San Telmo, you will hear tango music played to perfection. Food and drink are served but the centre's purpose is preserving tango as an art form rather than a tourist attraction. Regularly performing here are the remarkable Selección Nacional de Tango, an 18-member band, and resident singers Susana Rinaldi and Osvaldo Piro.
➕ H10 ✉ Defensa 1575 ☎ 4307-6506 🕐 Concerts at 10pm 🚇 Constitutión 💲 $30–$50

CONFITERÍA IDEAL

www.confiteriaideal.com

Nobody cares that this place is musty and dusty. Inside the faded grandeur of the belle-époque dining room and the upstairs ballroom delight locals and foreign visitors

alike. The tango shows are of the highest quality, sometimes with top musicians, singers and dancers vying for acclaim and applause.
🟥 G7 ✉ Suipacha 380 ☎ 5265-8069 🔘 Daily 9.30pm 🚇 Carlos Pellegrini (B), Diagonal Norte (C), 9 de Julio (D) 🚌 6, 7, 9, 10, 17, 23, 24, 26, 29, 45, 50, 70, 99, 109, 111, 142, 146, 155 💲 Shows $30, classes $30

CONGO

Although the leather interior of this leading Palermo bar is very cozy, the big advantage is the spotlit garden that has crowds waiting to get in after midnight. The other big attraction is the selection of fabulous cocktails—try the house special, the Bossa Nova, a near-lethal but delicious blend of rum, brandy, Galliano, passion fruit and honey.
🟥 A4 🟥 G8 ✉ Honduras 5329 ☎ 4833-5857 🔘 Mon–Sat from 8pm. Closed Sun 🚌 34, 55, 166

CONTRAMANO

www.contramano.com
The number of gay discos in the city is surprisingly small but Contramano is one of the major venues and throbs to electro sounds every weekend.
🟥 E6 ✉ Rodríguez Peña 1082 ☎ 4811-0494 🔘 Fri–Sat midnight–6am, Sun 10pm–5am 🚌 12, 30, 152 💲 Cover $30–$50 men, $70 women

ESQUINA HOMERO MANZI

www.esquinahomeromanzi.com.ar
Named for one of the great tango composers and musicians, this venerable institution offers private and group tango classes in the early evening before putting on one of the best dinner-shows in the city. The musicians and dancers give their all to make it a memorable evening. You can choose from three menus.
🟥 B10 ✉ Avenida San Juan 3601 ☎ 4957-8488 🔘 Tango classes 6–9pm; dinner 9pm; show 10pm 🚇 Boedo 💲 From $180

KIKA

www.kikaclub.com.ar
This popular club for over-21s only packs in the crowds thanks to its skilled DJs and danceable music. Doors open at 1.30 but things get going an hour or two later.
🟥 A4 ✉ Honduras 5339 ☎ 4137-5311 🔘 Tue–Sat from 1.30am. Closed Sun–Mon 🚌 34, 55, 166

MALUCO BELEZA

www.malucobeleza.com.ar
Salsa and samba are the beats at this dinner-dance club with a strong Brazilian flavour, where classes are given in addition to the popular dance shows.
🟥 F7 ✉ Sarmiento 1728 ☎ 4372-1737 🔘 Wed, Fri–Sat dinner show 10pm, club from 1.30am 🚌 12, 24, 26, 60, 146

The show at Esquina Homero Manzi

MANUFACTURA PAPELERA

www.manufacturapapelera.com.ar
An alternative opera, dance and theatre venue housed in a recycled San Telmo paper factory. The food is not that imaginative but decent nonetheless.

✚ H9 ✉ Bolívar 1582 ☎ 4361-8041
🕐 Thu–Sun 6pm, 8.30pm 🚌 24, 29, 39
💵 $5–$20

LA MARSHÁLL

www.lamarshall.com.ar
At this gay *milonga* you can dance with partners of the same sex, which apparently often happened in the early days of tango.

✚ G7 ✉ Avenida Independencia 571
☎ 4300-3487 🕐 Wed 10pm–3.30am
Ⓜ Independencia 💵 $30

MILIÓN

www.milion.com.ar
This glorious bar in ritzy Recoleta serves tapas along with an array of delicious drinks. On the first floor a refined restaurant serves Argentine dishes for dinner.

✚ F5 ✉ Paraná 1048 ☎ 4815-9925
🕐 Mon–Wed noon–2am, Thu noon–3am, Fri noon–4am, Sat 8pm–2am 🚌 29, 39, 152

A tango show at El Querandí

LA NACIONAL

This excellent *milonga* is held in the downtown Club Italiano and is one of the best venues for seeing and taking part in really authentic tango. Very popular with locals.

✚ F8 ✉ Alsina 1465 ☎ 4307-0146
🕐 Mon, Wed from 9pm, Sat 8pm–2am
Ⓜ Congreso 💵 $20

ND/ATENEO

www.ndateneo.com.ar
One of the best music venues, this attracts Argentina's leading rock, jazz, folk and tango performers to its regular Friday and Saturday concerts. Schedules may include poetry recitals, film screenings, drama performances or special evenings of techno-tango.

✚ G6 ✉ Paraguay 918 ☎ 4328-2888
🕐 Sun–Thu 10pm–late Ⓜ San Martín
💵 Check website

PACHÁ

www.pachabuenosaires.com
Multi-salons thronged with revellers, VIP lounges where champagne flows, starlit dance patios and terraces with views of the Río de la Plata, all help Pachá live up to its hedonistic reputation.

✚ D1 ✉ Avenida Rafael Obligado and La Pampa ☎ 4788-4280 🕐 Sat from 1am. Closed Jan 🚌 37, 160

PIAZZOLLA TANGO

www.piazzollatangoshow.com
Named after a great tango composer and *bandoneón* player, this majestic theatre is in the Galería Güemes. The dinner and tango shows are up there with the best.

✚ G7 ✉ Galería Güemes ☎ 4344-8201
🕐 Mon–Sun 9am–10pm Ⓜ Florida
💵 Show US$56–US$105, dinner and show US$100–US$140

EL QUERANDÍ

www.elquerandi.com.ar

This neocolonial building had an art deco facelift in the 1920s. After restoration in the 1990s it became a leading venue for tango shows. Its interior makes a fine setting for a tableaux aimed at the tourist, but the dancers, live musicians and choreography are excellent.

🔲 G8 ✉ Perú 302 ☎ 5199-1771 🕒 Daily lunch 12–4, dinner 8.30, show 10 🚇 Bolívar 🚌 Show US$62, dinner and show US$96

ROJO TANGO

www.rojotango.com

The tango show at Faena Hotel+Universe (▷ 156) is professional and sharp with live music by remarkable musicians.

🔲 J8 ✉ Martha Salotti 445 ☎ 5787-1536 🚇 Leandro N. Alem 🚌 2, 130, 152 🚌 Show US$50

SER SPA

www.aguaclubspa.com

You can indulge in pampering at this smart Palermo spa, in a beautiful Parisian-style town house.

🔲 C3 ✉ Cerviño 3626 ☎ 4807-4688 🕒 Mon–Fri 7.30–10.30, Sat 11–9, Sun, hols 12–8 🚇 Plaza Italia/Scalabrini Ortiz

TEATRO ASTRAL

www.teatroastral.com.ar

This is a classic Corrientes revue theatre staging Parisian-style cabaret with scantily clad models.

🔲 F7 ✉ Avenida Corrientes 1639 ☎ 4374-5707 🕒 Check website 🚇 Congreso, Callao 🚌 6, 12, 24, 37, 50, 60, 115, 124 🚌 $100–$150

TEATRO MAIPO

www.maipo.com.ar

The schedule at the illustrious Maipo ranges from cabaret to

revues and from tango to music concerts. Check the website for what's on and ticket prices.

🔲 G6 ✉ Esmeralda 443 ☎ 4322-4882 🚇 Lavalle

TEATRO MARGARITA XIRGU

www.margaritaxirgu.com

Named after a Catalan actress who made her name in Buenos Aires in the early 20th century, this theatre is worth a visit for the building alone—sumptuous neo-Gothic and art nouveau, with stained glass, ceramics and wrought-iron. Music and drama are mostly classical.

🔲 G7 ✉ Chacabuco 875 ☎ 4307-8817 🕒 Box office: Tue–Sun 2–8 🚇 Independencia 🚌 10, 17, 29, 59, 156

THELONIUS CLUB

www.thelonious.com.ar

Sip a cocktail at this top jazz venue listening to home-grown sounds and occasionally international big names from abroad. Thelonious has a mellow atmosphere and a lively schedule, with appearances by one of the best Argentine jazz groups, Escalandrum.

🔲 C4 ✉ Salguero 1884 ☎ 4829-1562 🕒 Wed–Sun from 9.30pm 🚇 Bulnes 🚌 $15

Eat

There are places to eat across the city to suit all tastes and budgets. In this section establishments are listed alphabetically.

EAT

Introduction

Residents are loyal to their Italian roots and favour pasta, pizza and *parrilla* (grilled beef)—after all, this is the world's steak capital. You will find other cuisines (Indian, Thai, Peruvian, Vietnamese and more) along with twists on traditional fare.

What to Eat

Vegetarianism is increasingly fashionable as Porteños try to cut down on meat, but they will find it strange if a visitor does not want to sample a juicy *bife de chorizo* (steak) during their stay. Remember, too, that Buenos Aires is close to the Atlantic—succulent fish and fresh seafood feature on a number of menus.

Where to Eat

Puerto Madero has some of the newest and most innovative restaurants, while Palermo Viejo sees a trendy *resto-bar* or deli sprout up every week. Recoleta and Retiro serve up haute cuisine and *parrillas*, while downtown is a melange of tourist rip-offs and bistros frequented by office workers. San Telmo can spring the odd surprise with some exclusive gourmet establishments.

Like mamma's

The city's Italian roots show up in the diet. Pasta is very popular, and tends to be filled with cheese and come with a tomato sauce. Gnocchi are an institution while classics like osso bucco and tiramisu are on many a menu.

PARRILLAS

The beef in Argentina is memorable so carnivores should definitely head for one of the city's myriad *parrillas*, where every part of the cow is served up in plentiful portions. The protocol usually entails a crescendo of meat quality, starting with cheaper cuts, including offal such as intestines and sweetbreads, and building up to the finest fillets. Vegetarians should steer clear.

From the top: Steak at La Cabrera restaurant; the café at the MALBA (▷ 38–39); empanadas are a popular snack; Natural Deli restaurant

Directory

City Centre

Cafés, Delis and Snacks
Café Tortoni
Florida Garden
Fine Dining
Tomo 1
Parrillas
Parrilla Peña
Vegetarian, Pasta and Pizza
Granix

Boca and San Telmo

Fine Dining
La Vinería de Gualterio Bolívar
International
Caseros
Sagardi Euskal Taberna
Parrillas
La Brigada
El Obrero
Vegetarian, Pasta and Pizza
Orígen
Il Piccolo Vapore

Retiro and Recoleta

Cafés, Delis and Snacks
La Biela
Cumaná
El Sanjuanino
Fine Dining
La Bourgogne
International
Empire Thai
Oviedo
Sirop and Sirop Folie
Tancat
Tandoor
Pasta and Pizza
El Cuartito
Filo

Palermo

Cafés, Delis and Snacks
b-Blue Deli and Natural Bar
Mark's Deli
Un'Altra Volta

Fine Dining
Freud Y Fahler
Tegui
International
Azema Exotic Bistró
Bereber
La Fábrica del Taco
Ølsen
Pozo Santo
Sudestada
Xalapa
Parrillas
La Cabrera
Don Julio
Vegetarian, Pasta and Pizza
Buenos Aires Verde

Puerto Madero

Cafés, Delis and Snacks
I Fresh Market
Fine Dining
Ayres de Patagonia
El Bistro
Cabaña Las Lilas
Chila
Parrillas
Siga La Vaca
Vegetarian, Pasta and Pizza
Bice
Sottovoce

Further Afield

Cafés, Delis and Snacks
Meraviglia
Fine Dining
Casa Félix
Vegetarian, Pasta and Pizza
Arevalito
Il Novo Maria Luján del Tigre

EAT

PRICES

Prices are approximate, based on a three-course meal for one person.

$$$ over $30
$$ $15–$30
$ under $15

AYRES DE PATAGONIA $$$

www.airesdepatagonia.com
This swish restaurant will transport you to Patagonia via your taste-buds. The extensive menu features specialties such as lake trout and baby lamb, along with some superb Sauvignon Blancs and marvellous Malbecs from the world's most southerly vineyards.
🔲 A2 ⊠ Alicia Moreau de Justo 1798 ☎ 4315-2151 ⏰ Fri–Sat 12–1, Sun–Thu 12–12 🚇 Leandro N. Alem

AREVALITO $$

This tiny meatless bistro luckily has some outdoor seating, otherwise it would never have room for all the eager customers chomping at the bit for one of the day's half dozen specials. There is always at least one home-made pasta dish on the

PRICE AND MEAL TIMES

Eating out in Buenos Aires is pleasing to the palate and easy on the wallet, costing far less than in comparable cities around the world. You can breakfast for around $15, enjoy a fixed lunch (*menú ejecutivo*) for as little as $35 and dine for under $60. Even so, more exclusive restaurants charge upwards of $150–$200 a head, without counting wine. Porteños eat late: between 1 and 3pm for lunch while dinner is seldom before 9pm; many diners turn up at restaurants as late as midnight.

blackboard, while crisp salads with unusual ingredients always please.
🔲 A2 ⊠ Arévalo 1478 ☎ 4776-4252 ⏰ Mon–Fri 9am–midnight, Sat 10–5. Closed Sun 🚇 Borrego (B) 🚌 39, 93, 111, 140, 151, 161

AZEMA EXOTIC BISTRÓ $$$

Azema takes an eclectic approach to cuisine. Its menu encompasses dishes from France with touches from Polynesia and North Africa, plus the Île de le Réunion in the Indian Ocean where Monsieur Azema has his own origins.
🔲 A3 ⊠ Ángel Carranza 1875 ☎ 4774-4191 ⏰ Mon–Sat 8pm–12. Closed Sun 🚌 39, 93, 111, 161

B-BLUE DELI AND NATURAL BAR $

www.b-blue.com.ar
The name refers to blueberries and the fact that this place is run by a blueberry grower. Blueberries (*arándanos*) thrive in Argentina and here they are put to great use in fruity muffins and creamy smoothies, as well as in ultra-fresh salads and inventive sandwiches. The coffee is excellent, too, and there is a much sought-after patio.
🔲 A4 ⊠ Armenia 1692 ☎ 4831-7024 ⏰ Daily 9am–10pm 🚌 15, 55, 57

BEREBER $$

Moroccan food is a rarity in Buenos Aires but this authentically decorated place makes up for that. Star-shaped lanterns give a mellow light, while there is also a terrace overlooking the plaza. Salads of Mediterranean vegetables and North African spices are a treat.
🔲 A4 ⊠ Armenia 1880 ☎ 4833-5662 ⏰ Daily 8.30pm–12. Closed Sat–Sun 🚇 Plaza Italia 🚌 39, 55

BICE $$$

www.bicebuenosaires.com

Fresh antipasti and rich lasagne are mainstays at this Italian restaurant, where chef Pablo Mazza uses the best ingredients. In a converted Madero warehouse, it has a mellow decor. Service is exceptional.

➕ J6 ✉ Alicia Moreau de Justo 192 ☎ 4315-6219 🕐 12–4, 8–1 🚇 Leandro N. Alem

LA BIELA $$

www.labiela.com

A *confitería* (▷ 145, panel), this is opposite the entrance to Recoleta cemetery. It is worth the 20 per cent mark-up to people-watch under a *gomero* (rubber tree) on the terrace. Try the special of *lomo Biela*, slices of grilled beef in crusty bread, served with French fries.

➕ E4 ✉ Avenida Quintana 600 ☎ 4804-0432 🕐 Daily 7am–3pm 🚌 10, 17, 60, 67, 92, 110

EL BISTRO $$$

www.faenahotelanduniverse.com

The Faena Hotel+Universe (▷ 156) is full of surprises, not least this extravagant dining room designed by Philippe Starck, with its famous unicorn heads on the walls. Chef Mariano Cid de la Paz produces the likes of octopus salad with grilled fruit and vegetables or lamb steak with smoked aubergine (eggplant) couscous.

➕ J8 ✉ Martha Salotti 445 ☎ 4010-9200 🕐 Wed–Sat 8pm–12. Closed Sun–Tue 🚇 Leandro N. Alem 🚌 2, 130, 152

LA BOURGOGNE $$$

www.alvearpalace.com

For refined French cooking using the best Argentine ingredients—famous pampas beef, delicious rabbit, fresh sea bream—married with one of the best cellars in the city, think seriously about reserving a table at this famous restaurant in the great Alvear Palace (▷ 156).

➕ F4 ✉ Avenida Alvear 1891 ☎ 4804-2100 🕐 Mon–Fri 12–3.30, 7–12, Sat 7–12. Closed Sun 🚌 67, 93, 130

LA BRIGADA $$

La Brigada prides itself on being one of the city's best *parrillas* and when you tuck into a juicy steak

Bice Italian restaurant is in a trendy converted warehouse building

you'll find it hard to argue. The decor is deliberately rustic, with whitewashed brick walls and a host of black-and-white photos of the *barrio* in days of yore. They have an exceptional wine list to match the beef.

⊞ H9 ✉ Estados Unidos 465 ☎ 4361-5557 ⏰ Sun–Thu 12–3, 8–12, Fri-Sat 12–4, 8–1 🚌 29, 126, 195

BUENOS AIRES VERDE $$

www.bsasverde.com

This excellent little vegetarian place has some tables outside, and is an appealing place to try good meat-less cuisine. The cereal-rich breads are baked on the premises and the fruit juices are freshly squeezed. Imaginative salads and quiches are the mainstays.

⊞ H9 ✉ Gorriti 5657 ☎ 4775-9594 ⏰ Mon–Sat 9am–midnight 🚇 Palermo 🚌 9, 11

CABAÑA LAS LILAS $$$

www.laslilas.com

Expensive and touristy, Las Lilas is the classic Puerto Madero haunt and is no rip-off. The owners have their own cattle ranch and the slabs of sirloin and rib-eye steaks are perfectly grilled. Kick off with a carpaccio of Portobello mushrooms and finish with a perfect tarte tatin with cinnamon ice cream. Service is impeccable and the wine list is unimpeachable.

⊞ H6 ✉ Alicia Moreau de Justo 192 ☎ 4315-1010 ⏰ Daily noon–1am 🚇 Leandro N. Alem

LA CABRERA $$

www.parrillalacabrera.com.ar

It is not easy to make a reservation at this excellent corner-house *parrilla*, or its younger sister, La Cabrera Norte, a few doors up, so you might just have to wait outside in this leafy part of Palermo Viejo and sip champagne until a table frees up. The quality and size of the *bife de chorizo* (sirloin steak) are overwhelming and while you wait for them to sizzle you can sample delicious tapas—butter beans and aubergine salad, tiny potatoes and cherry tomatoes—served in little china pots.

⊞ A4 ✉ Cabrera 5099/5127 ☎ 4831-7002/4832-5754 ⏰ Fri-Sat 12.30–4.30, 8–2, Sun–Thu 12.30–4.30, 8–1.30 🚌 39, 55

CAFÉ TORTONI $$

www.cafetortoni.com.ar

The Tortoni is more a national monument than a café but you can lap up the ambience of early 20th-century Buenos Aires, admiring the beautiful stained glass and polished wood panelling. Downstairs in the bodega there are regular tango shows aimed at the tourist market.

⊞ G7 ✉ Avenida de Mayo 825 ☎ 4342-4328 ⏰ Mon–Thu 8am–2am, Fri-Sat 8am–3am, Sun 9am–1am 🚇 Piedras (A) 🚌 17, 64, 86

CASA FÉLIX $$$

www.colectivofelix.com

It is worth the trek out to Chacarita for this *puertas cerradas* (closed doors) establishment and its exciting meat-free fare concocted by Diego Félix. He travels around the Americas in search of new ingredients and novel ideas, before transposing them to an intimate suburban kitchen. In the tiny dining room a lucky few can taste unusual dishes such as the rocket and spinach salad with dressing and grilled *surubí* (local fish) with *manioc* (cassava) and *aguaribay* (peppery spice).

⊞ I12 **✉** Call for directions and travel information **☎** 4555-1882 **◷** Thu, Fri and Sat dinner, reservations only

CASEROS $$

www.caserosrestaurante.com.ar

Tucked away near San Telmo's Parque Lezama, this unpretentious bistro serves French-influenced cuisine using harvest-fresh goods from the market. Its bright white decor is enhanced by the huge windows that offer views on to the avenue outside. A typical *menú del día* might include a couscous salad then steak with carrots and fennel.

⊞ H10 **✉** Avenida Caseros 486 **☎** 4307-4729 **◷** Tue–Sat 12.30–3.30, 8.30–12.30. Closed Sun–Mon **🚌** 10, 29, 39, 70,195

CHILA $$$

www.chilaweb.com.ar

Chila is synonymous with elegance and fulfils its mission to make guests feel special as they enjoy a gourmet experience. The simple, yet sophisticated dishes include rabbit and morel ravioli or black risotto with seafood and lumpfish roe. Hundreds of vintages grace the cellar—take the opportunity to try a Luigi Bosca 2006 Malbec.

⊞ H6 **✉** Alicia Moreau de Justo 1160 **☎** 4343-6067 **◷** Daily 12–4, 7–1 **🚌** 2, 103, 152, 195

EL CUARTITO $

Buenos Aires has hundreds of *pizzerías* to choose from but this Barrio Norte address is a classic. El Cuartito endlessly churns out crusty pizzas with generous toppings, from classic margaritas to *fugazza* (a South American pizza) with mozzarella, plus juicy

empanadas (stuffed pastry) from the wood-fired oven. There is a lively hubbub, brisk service and a rough-and-ready ambience of blaring soccer on the TV, glaring neons and formica tables, for which you might have to wait.

⊞ F6 **✉** Talcahuano 937 **☎** 4816-1758 **◷** Daily noon–1am **🚇** Tribunales

CUMANÁ $

This laid-back traditional joint is a great place in the city to take a break from sophisticated gourmet fare and try some *criollo* (rural Argentine) specialties like *empanadas* (pasties filled with chopped steak) and *locro* (a filling stew of beans and corn). Drop in one afternoon to taste *mate* (a traditional infusion) with pastries.

⊞ E6 **✉** Rodríguez Peña 1149 **☎** 4813-9207 **◷** Daily noon–1am **🚌** 10, 12, 31, 37, 39, 101, 124, 132, 150, 152

DON JULIO $$

Leather tablecloths and bare brick walls lined with row upon row of empty wine bottles signed by customers—locals and tourists alike—are the setting for this not-to-be-missed Palermo *parrilla*. This is the kind of steak temple where you might consider not sharing the

EAT

sirloin *(bife de chorizo)* after all, even though it covers the plate. Pumpkin and spinach soufflé is just one of the vegetarian dishes served. The expert waiters can help you choose a wine from the extensive bodega list.

🚼 A4 ✉ Guatemala 4691 ☎ 4831-9564 🕙 Daily 12–4, 7.30–1 🚍 35, 55, 93, 111, 161

EMPIRE THAI $$

www.empirethai.net

A stylish establishment in a quiet pedestrianized side street in Retiro, striving to combine New York sophistication with Asian fusion food. The sleek decor of mirror mosaics and backlit bar and the delicious spicy green curries are a winning combination.

🚼 H6 ✉ Tres Sargentos 427 ☎ 4312-5706 🕙 Mon–Fri 12–12, Sat 7pm–2am. Closed Sat lunch and Sun 🚇 San Martín 🚍 93, 152

LA FÁBRICA DEL TACO $

www.lafabricadeltaco.com

Taco factory by name and by nature, this unpretentious and

A submarino cocktail

gloriously kitsch Mexican bar-cum-restaurant churns out tacos with traditional fillings by the dozen. The quesadillas are delicious and of course there is guacamole by the bucketful. Mexican-style hamburgers bring in the crowds, too.

🚼 A4 ✉ Gorriti 5062 ☎ 4833-3534 🕙 Tue–Sun 1pm till late. Closed Mon 🚍 15, 55, 57, 140, 151, 168

FILO $$

www.filo-ristorante.com

This busy Italian restaurant seldom empties, with a stream of eager diners bumping into each other in the late afternoon. This is a noisy boisterous place, with glam waiting staff and a blaring sound system. Don't come here to linger over food, but wolf down a delicious pizza while listening to jazz or rock. The minestrone soup and generous salads are great, too.

🚼 C6 ✉ San Martín 975 ☎ 4311-0312 🕙 Daily 12–4, 8–2 🚇 San Martín 🚍 10, 93, 130, 152

FLORIDA GARDEN $

For some 1960s' nostalgia and a decent coffee, look no further than this landmark corner-house *confitería*, with efficient waiters in impeccable white jackets, serving house specials, such as tomato and turkey sandwiches with glasses of ice-cold beer. It's a great place for people-watching, at the chic end of the busy Calle Florida.

🚼 G6 ✉ Florida 899 ☎ 4312-7902 🕙 Mon–Fri 6am–midnight, Sat 6am–11pm, Sun 8am–11pm 🚇 San Martín

FREUD Y FAHLER $$

On an inviting corner, this modern restaurant has an appealing simple decor set off by red walls and sparkling chandeliers. The staff are very friendly. The food is sketched out with mathematical precision on a clever menu, and is prepared with incisive skill by the chef. Dishes are often based on unusual ingredients, such as llama steaks, beet leaves and plums (a much under-used fruit in Argentina).

🔲 A4 ✉ Gurruchaga 1750 ☎ 4833-2153 🕐 Mon–Sat 12.30–3.30, 8.30–12. Closed Sun 🚌 39, 55

GRANIX $

The variety of salads and vegetarian dishes, mostly based on native ingredients such as quinoa and squash, at this fixed-charge health-food restaurant are great value. Buy a ticket at the entrance, on the first floor of one of the city's best shopping arcades, take a tray, and fill up with asparagus quiche, sweetcorn au gratin and carrot soufflé plus fruit-based drinks and healthy desserts, such as home-made flan.

🔲 G7 ✉ Florida 165 ☎ 4343-4020 🕐 Mon–Fri 11am–3pm 🚇 Florida, Catedral

I FRESH MARKET $$

www.icentralmarket.com.ar

This quality deli also serves great food and has the advantage of a terrace overlooking the docks. You might choose a light salad with a honey and blue-cheese dressing or a risotto with grilled peppers, mint and feta cheese, or maybe stir-fried chicken with cashew nuts, aubergines (eggplant) and courgettes (zucchini) served with rice. If you like the crockery you can buy a set inside the store.

🔲 J7 ✉ Azucena Villaflor 340 ☎ 5775-0330 🕐 Daily 8am–midnight 🚌 2, 102, 152, 195

MARK'S DELI $$

www.markspalermo.com

Sometimes Buenos Aires is a wannabe New York and the rise of the deli is definitely part of that yearning. Mark's Deli, on one of the hippest corners of Palermo Soho, has the requisite soothing orange decor and smiley staff, while the smoked salmon bagels and tangy home-made lemonade approach Manhattan levels of authenticity.

🔲 A4 ✉ El Salvador 4701 ☎ 4832-6244 🕐 Mon–Sat 8.30–9.30, Sun 10.30–9 🚌 15, 39, 55

MERAVIGLIA $$

www.meraviglia.com.ar

This wonderfully informal deli-cum-café is one of the best places in town for seeking out veggie delights. Owner Mariana Chami claims that avoiding meat helped to cure her arthritis, while celebrity chef López May is known across the continent for her inventive cooking using fruit, vegetables and grains. A great place for healthy breakfasts, it also serves excellent diet-conscious lunches.

🔲 A4 ✉ Gorriti 5796 ☎ 4633-7403 🕐 Mon–Sat 9–8 🚇 Palermo

IL NOVO MARÍA LUJÁN DEL TIGRE $$$

www.ilnovomariadellujan.com

Occupying pride of place on the Río Luján, with a terrace to take in the riverside views, this is an old Tigre chestnut. The elegant peach-walled dining-room, white-clothed tables and handsome wooden chairs are the perfect setting for fine Italian cuisine—crab ravioli in squid ink or veal escalopes in marsala sauce, with charlottes, ice creams and zabaglione for dessert.

112 ✉ Paseo Victorica 611 ☎ 4731-9613 🕐 Daily 12–4, 8–12 🚃 Tigre

EL OBRERO $

Founded decades ago by two Catalan brothers, El Obrero is now one of the most popular *parrillas* in Boca, and the patrons' loyalty to their football team is reflected in all the Boca Juniors memorabilia here. Steak and chicken dominate the menu; you can ask for small portions if you want to share the dishes, which are generously filled.
J11 ✉ Agustín Caffarena 64 ☎ 4362-9912 🕐 Mon–Sat 1–4, 8–1. Closed Sun 🚃 25, 29, 68, 130

ØLSEN $$$

The Scandinavian theme goes all the way from the pine-grove and minimalist sculptures in the front garden to the vodka shots that accompany the food—everything has a pared-down Swedish feel. A fabulous place for Sunday brunch, hyper-trendy Olsen specializes in cured and smoked meats and fish, such as Patagonian trout with blinis. Its barstaff shake some of the best cocktails in the city.
A4 ✉ Gorriti 5870 ☎ 4776-7677 🕐 Tue–Sat 12.30pm–1am, Sun 10.30am–midnight. Closed Mon 🚃 39, 93, 111, 161

ORÍGEN $$$

This wholefood resto-bar does wholegrain pizzas topped with sautéed vegetables, fruit smoothies and other vegetarian delights, making this friendly café a real find. The menu is a bit limited but non-meat eaters will appreciate the pumpkin ravioli, stir-fried vegetables with bamboo, tofu and almonds, and the lentil, rice, potato and pumpkin stew.
H9 ✉ Humberto Primo 599 ☎ 4362-7979 🕐 Mon–Tue 9am–4pm, Wed–Sun 9am–1am 🚇 San Juan (C) 🚃 22, 24, 45, 74, 86, 126

OVIEDO $$$

www.oviedoresto.com.ar
Sophisticated Spanish gastronomy is what Oviedo does best, in a stylish restaurant with a handsome mosaic floor, starched tablecloths and attentive waiters. The fish and seafood are brought fresh from Mar del Plata and the wine list includes outstanding Chardonnays served by the glass.
D5 ✉ Beruti 2602 ☎ 4821-3741 🕐 Mon–Sat 12–3.30, 8–1. Closed Sun 🚇 Pueyrredón (D) 🚃 12, 64, 152

PARRILLA PEÑA $$

This is a traditional neighbourhood *parrilla* in downtown San Nicolás with white tablecloths and old-fashioned waiters who will tell you which wine to have with the succulent *bife de chorizo* (sirloin) or the crispy *tira de asado* (ribs).

EAT

Let your *mozo* (waiter) dress a delicious salad with olive oil and balsamic vinegar.

🚇 E6 ✉ Rodríguez Peña 682 ☎ 4371-5643 🕐 Mon–Sat 12–4, 8–12. Sun 12–4 🚇 Callao (B/D)

IL PICCOLO VAPORE $$

www.ilpiccolovapore.com

Il Piccolo Vapore is one of the last of Boca's traditional Italian *cantinas* —don't be put off by the kitsch exterior (a mural of a steamship) or the garish interior. It is a great place for fried squid and roast chicken, perfectly cooked pasta and delicious ice cream. The house wine flows liberally. Earthy musical cabaret and dance shows often accompany the set dinner.

🚇 J11 ✉ Necochea 1190 ☎ 4301-4455 🕐 Daily 11–8 🚌 25, 29, 68

POZO SANTO $$$

www.pozosanto.com.ar

This restaurant is the best of many top-end Peruvian restaurants in the city, combining a luxurious decor (colonial artwork and rustic handicrafts on the wall) and exciting

Andean cuisine. Chef Rafael Danila prepares tantalizing *ceviche* (marinated fish with chilli), a fabulous *ají de gallina* (spicy chicken stew) and simple grilled tuna with stir-fried vegetables.

🚇 A4 ✉ El Salvador 4968 ☎ 4833-1711 🕐 Mon–Sat 12–3, 8–late. Closed Sun 🚌 15, 55, 57, 110

SAGARDI EUSKAL TABERNA $$$

www.sagardi.com.ar

Taking its inspiration from traditional Basque cider breweries, this cutting-edge tavern produces an amazing variety of fabulous *pintxos* —Basque bite-sized tapas—that go well with the excellent wine, beer and cider served on tap.

🚇 H9 ✉ Humberto Primo 319 ☎ 4361-2538 🕐 Daily 1–4, 8–12 🚌 10, 22, 24, 45

EL SANJUANINO $

www.elsanjuanino.com

There are three branches of this mini-chain in the city but this is the best and most central. The house special is *empanada*, with a range of fillings from the usual meat to

Scandinavian style at Ølsen

Smorgasbord and vodka are on the menu at Ølsen

ham and cheese, sweetcorn, chicken, mixed vegetables, mozzarella, tomato and basil or Roquefort-style cheese. Other dishes are national favourites originating in the Andean northwest of the country, mostly based on corn.
🚩 F4 ✉ Posadas 1515 ☎ 4804-2902 🕐 Daily 12–4, 7–1 🚇 Callao

SIGA LA VACA $$–$$$

www.sigalavaca.com

The name means 'follow the cow' and you do just that—look for the emblematic animal guarding the entrance. Part of a citywide chain, this all-included *parrilla*—a massive mixed grill of beef and pork—varies its price according to the time of day and day of the week.
🚩 H6 ✉ Alicia Moreau de Justo 1714 ☎ 4315-6801 🕐 Daily noon–1am 🚇 Leandro N. Alem

SIROP AND SIROP FOLIE $$

www.siroprestaurant.com

The name gives it away—this duo of restaurants in a Parisian-style alley aim for sophisticated French fare, though the Sunday brunches at Sirop Folie offer the full works *à l'américaine*.
🚩 F5 ✉ Vicente López 1661 ☎ 4813-5900 🕐 Mon–Fri 12–3.30, 8–12, Sat 8pm–12. Brunch Sat–Sun 11–4 🚌 37, 124

SOTTOVOCE $$$

www.sottovoceristorante.com.ar

This much-loved Italian restaurant has a branch in Recoleta but the Puerto Madero venue is a good place to try Mediterranean food at its best. In a stylish setting with diffused lighting and a smart wooden bar, Sottovoce is known for its discreet professional service and succulent fresh pasta.
🚩 H6 ✉ Alicia Moreau de Justo 176 ☎ 4313-1199 🕐 Daily 12–4, 8.30–1 🚌 26, 109, 129, 140

SUDESTADA $$$

www.sudestadabuenosaires.com

At this scintillating Palermo Soho corner-house you can start with a cocktail based on a Korean rice spirit to prepare your taste buds for the spicy food. Start with steamed dumplings, then try the curries, stir-fries or noodles. The star dish is *nem cua*, crisp pork and shrimp spring rolls. It's a tiny venue, so reservations are essential.
🚩 A4 ✉ Guatemala 5602 ☎ 4776-3777 🕐 Mon–Sat 12–3.30, 8–1. Closed Sun 🚉 Palermo (D) 🚌 15, 55, 111

TANCAT $$$

This is a bit of Barcelona's *Ramblas* thrown into downtown Retiro—the Hispanic decor and guitar music set the scene for delicious tapas. Sangria and draught beer in small glasses transport you to the Costa Brava as do the succulent baby squid and grilled fish. The place gets busy with office workers at lunchtime but is quieter for dinner.
🚩 G6 ✉ Paraguay 645 ☎ 4312-5442 🕐 Mon–Sat noon–1am. Closed Sun 🚉 San Martín

TANDOOR $$$

www.tandoor.com.ar

This smart Recoleta restaurant has won the Indian embassy's seal of approval with its curries and naan bread. Succulent Patagonian lamb is alchemically transformed into an aromatic curry while the chicken tikka masala is a firm favourite.
🚩 C5 ✉ Laprida 1293 ☎ 4821-3676 🕐 Daily 12–4, 8–1 🚉 Agüero (D) 🚌 12, 39, 64, 152

TEGUI $$$

www.tegui.com.ar

Black-and-white decor behind a trendily tagged facade—ring the bell to get in—is a sure sign you are in the city's trendiest restaurant, chef supremo Germán Martitegui's latest venture in Palermo Soho. As at his other restaurant, Casa Cruz, the wine cellar takes up a whole wall, while the open kitchen lets you see the chefs as they produce nouvelle cuisine extravaganzas.

🕂 A4 ✉ Costa Rica 5852 ☎ 5291-3333 🕙 Tue–Sat 12–3, 8–12. Closed Sun and Mon 🚌 34, 55, 108

TOMO 1 $$$

www.tomo1.com.ar

Tomo 1, in the Panamericano hotel in downtown, is a landmark restaurant, the ideal place for a special-occasion meal. It remains traditional and the service is unmatched in the city. The pear, watercress and brie salad is a great way to start, maybe followed by gigot of Patagonian lamb with braised artichoke hearts.

🕂 G6 ✉ Carlos Pellegrini 521 ☎ 4326-6698 🕙 Mon–Fri 12–3, 7.30–1, Sat 7.30–1. Closed Sun 🚇 Carlos Pellegrini 🚌 10, 17, 29

UN'ALTRA VOLTA $

www.unaltravolta.com.ar

Luscious brownies are reasons in themselves to visit one of the smart branches of this stylish chain. However, the real draws are the fabulous ice cream flavours: a dozen different chocolate varieties, including the house special with Piemontese hazelnuts, tangy lemon or tangerine, but best of all seven heavenly kinds of dulce de leche (caramel).

🕂 C3 ✉ Avenida Libertador 3060 ☎ 4783-4048 🕙 Daily 10am–1am 🚌 10, 34, 130

LA VINERÍA DE GUALTERIO BOLÍVAR $$$

www.lavineriadegualteriobolivar.com

This highly sophisticated wine bar conjures up refined dishes to accompany carefully picked wines. The chefs are experts in molecular cooking—invented in Spain and now all the rage in Argentina. The tasting menu is a work of art.

🕂 H9 ✉ Bolívar 865 ☎ 4361-4709 🕙 Tue–Sun 12–4, 9–1. Closed Mon 🚇 Independencia (C) 🚌 24, 29

XALAPA $$

Mexican food is very popular in Buenos Aires, though it is really more like Tex-Mex in terms of authenticity. This bright corner joint with zingy orange walls and friendly staff mixes a mean margarita and follows up with a good range of Mexican dishes; a favourite is the spicy pollo con mole, chicken in chocolate sauce.

🕂 A4 ✉ El Salvador 4800 ☎ 4833-6102 🕙 Closed weekend evenings 🚌 39, 55

PARRILLA PICKS

With Argentine beef the best in the world, the barbecue is a key part of Porteño life. Whether prepared at home (the asado) or at a parrilla (grill house), a huge cow fest will be on the agenda during any visit to the city. Traditionally the whole beast is savoured, starting with crispy sweetbreads (mollejas) or chubby chorizo sausages and limbering up through the cheaper cuts like tira de asado (ribs), culminating in the delicate lomo (fillet) and doorstep bife de chorizo (sirloin). No condiments should be necessary.

Sleep

Ranging from luxurious and modern upmarket hotels to simple budget hotels, Buenos Aires has accommodation to suit everyone. In this section establishments are listed alphabetically.

SLEEP

Introduction

Buenos Aires has historic palace hotels whose guests have included Madonna and the King of Spain, but with the boom in international tourism a new generation of lodgings has widened the choice of places to stay in nearly every *barrio*.

Location

Decide which part of the city offers what most interests you and opt to stay there. Palermo is great for its open spaces and bars, restaurants and boutiques, and in Palermo Soho there is at least one trendy boutique hotel on every block. In Retiro, Recoleta and the downtown hotels are more mainstream, while many of San Telmo's 19th-century mansions are now characterful hotels and hostels. Puerto Madero hosts excitingly contemporary hotels whereas the city centre is more business-oriented.

Hotels

Five-star hotels are dotted around the *barrios* but more intimate places fall into two main categories: the boutique hotels, mostly but not exclusively, in Palermo Soho and less self-conscious B&Bs in San Telmo and the city centre. Free WiFi or internet, small plunge pools, sundecks and patios are all commonplace, but spas can be hit and miss.

APARTMENTS

Even if you are planning on staying only a couple of days you might like to opt for a furnished apartment rather than a hotel. Several reputable companies offer a range of short-term rentals over the internet, some specializing in family travel, services for gay and lesbian travellers or luxury residences.

www.buenosaireshabitat.com
www.oasisba.com
www.ba4uapartments.com.ar
www.bairesapartments.com
www.buenosairesapartments.com

From the top: Hotel Madero; hotel reception; one of the public areas in Hotel Madero; a Recoleta youth hostel

Directory

City Centre

Budget
Milhouse
Posada de la Luna
Mid-Range
1890 Hotel Boutique
Casa Calma
Rooney's

Boca and San Telmo

Budget
Ostinatto
Mid-Range
Moreno
Ribera Sur
Luxury
Mansión Vitraux

Retiro and Recoleta

Luxury
Algodón Mansion
Alvear Palace
Casa Sur

Palermo

Mid-Range
Craft
Five Cool Rooms
Home
Magnolia
Mine
Tailor Made Hotel
Ultra
Luxury
Legado Mítico

Puerto Madero

Luxury
Faena Hotel+Universe
Hotel Madero

Further Afield

Mid-Range
Bauen

Sleeping A–Z

PRICES

Prices are approximate and based on per night for a double room.

$$$	over US$250
$$	US$100–US$250
$	under US$100

1890 HOTEL BOUTIQUE $$

www.1890hotel.com.ar

This late-19th-century downtown mansion houses a romantic little hotel with only six suites, all of which look on to a beautiful patio and have names like Honeysuckle and White Camellia. All the suites are air conditioned and have WiFi.
✉ F9 ✉ Salta 1074 ☎ 4304-7385 🚇 San Juan

ALGODÓN MANSION $$$

www.algodonmansion.com

The beautiful Chez Nous dining room and Cognac Bar set the scene at this newcomer among the Porteño 5-stars in a 1912 Recoleta mansion. At le Spa you can try wine treatments using produce from the owners' San Rafael vineyards while the furnishing in the rooms is straight out of glossy interior design magazines.
✉ F5 ✉ Montevideo 1647 ☎ 3530-7777 🚇 San Martín

ALVEAR PALACE $$$

www.alvearpalace.com

If you want to stay in the best Buenos Aires hotel, then the Alvear Palace is the place for you. All 197 rooms and suites reflect the elegance that earned the city its nickname of 'Paris of the South', with their Empire, Louis XV and Louis XVI decor and exclusive Argentine art collection.

✉ F4 ✉ Avenida Alvear 1891 ☎ 4808-2100 🚌 67, 93, 130

BAUEN $$

www.bauenhotel.com.ar

An interesting example of a hotel run by its employees following the 2001 crisis, Bauen is a great value-for-money 4-star at an excellent position in the theatre district. The decor of its 186 rooms is modern and functional.

✉ E7 ✉ Avenida Callao 360 ☎ 4373-9009 🚇 Callao

CASA CALMA $$

www.casacalma.com.ar

An oasis of calm in the bustling downtown, the environmentally friendly Casa Calma takes the spa hotel concept all the way—instead of leaving your room for the wellness facilities, you stay put and make use of the Jacuzzi, sauna and organic health products.

✉ G5 ✉ Suipacha 1015 ☎ 5199-2800 🚇 San Martín (C) 🚌 17, 59, 61, 62, 75, 92, 100, 130, 152

CASA SUR $$$

www.casasurhotel.com

Recoleta is known for its patrician flair and sophistication and the Casa Sur Art Hotel fits in perfectly. L'Occitane toiletries, pillow menus and a zen-like spa are three of the attractions of this superb establishment with 36 spacious and luxurious rooms.

✉ F4 ✉ Avenida Callao 1823 ☎ 4515-0085 🚌 17, 59, 67, 75

CRAFT $$

www.crafthotel.com

Calling itself hip, the Craft is certainly designed to impress. Minimalist and quirky also describe this small hotel where services include use of bicycles, free WiFi and an excellent buffet breakfast, all in a fabulous setting overlooking one of the leafiest squares in Palermo Soho.

✉ A4 ✉ Nicaragua 4583 ☎ 4833-0060 🚌 34, 36, 55, 93, 161

FAENA HOTEL+UNIVERSE $$$

www.faenahotelanduniverse.com

Alan Faena's idiosyncratic Puerto Madero hotel, with 66 rooms, four studios and eight suites, has won countless awards for being hip, cool, groundbreaking and simply luxurious. Housed in a converted warehouse, it is best known for its white-decorated restaurant El Bistro (▷ 143). El Cabaret puts on a highly acclaimed tango show.

BED AND BREAKFAST

In Buenos Aires there are two ways to be chic—imitate French elegance and savoir-faire or ape British tradition and intimate charm. B&Bs fall into the latter category but, whereas in Anglo-Saxon cultures the term denotes family homes taking in guests, in Buenos Aires they tend to be elegant and up-market, with prices to match, mostly falling into the middle range. Often it is hard to tell them apart from the now-ubiquitous boutique hotels, with their smart decor and mini-spas.

✉ J8 ✉ Martha Salotti 445 ☎ 4010-9000
🚇 Leandro N. Alem 🚌 2, 130, 152

FIVE COOL ROOMS $$
www.fivebuenosaires.com
The name of this Palermo Soho hideout says it all. Five impeccably designed suites, varying from small to extra large, give you access to a fabulous chill-out terrace with a Jacuzzi and barbecue facilities. There are also 11 rooms with good facilities, including free WiFi and bicycle rental.
✉ A4 ✉ Honduras 4742 ☎ 5235-5555
🚌 39, 93

HOME $$
www.homebuenosaires.com
This home-from-home Palermo hotel even offers you two lofts, if rooms are not enough, with gorgeous contemporary decor plus a fully equipped kitchen and dining area so you can do a spot of self-catering. The twice-daily maid service makes sure everything stays perfectly clean.
✉ A4 ✉ Honduras 5860 ☎ 4778-1008
🚌 39, 93, 111

HOTEL MADERO $$$
www.hotelmadero.com
With its tricolour trio of Red Resto and Lounge, White Bar and Blue Sky Bar, the Madero, named for the trendy *barrio* where it is found, has just about all its guests could wish for, once you have factored in the M Club, an exclusive service including a butler, mobile phone loan and a personal secretary.
✉ I9 ✉ Rosario Vera Peñaloza 360
☎ 5776-7700 🚇 Leandro N. Alem
🚌 2, 130, 152

LEGADO MÍTICO $$$
www.legadomitico.com
Among Palermo Soho's many great places to stay, this stands out. Its themed rooms, spacious and impeccably furnished, are dedicated to figures such as Che Guevara, Evita, Carlos Gardel (▷ 73) and cartoon character, Mafalda, but professionalism, elegance and comfort win out over gimmickry and whimsy. The library has tourist information.
✉ A4 ✉ Gurruchaga 1848 ☎ 4833-1300
🚌 39, 55, 93, 152

SLEEP

Moreno hotel (▷ 158)

A room in Hotel Madero

MAGNOLIA $$

www.magnoliahotel.com.ar

This exquisite gem, not quite in the trendiest sector of Palermo, manages to be welcoming and discreet, luxurious and unpretentious—in short it is one of the best of its kind, with three categories of rooms (Terraza, Patio and Vitraux), all furnished with handpicked items and decorated in the best possible taste. All rooms have WiFi and air conditioning.

🔢 B5 ✉ Julián Álvarez 1746 ☎ 4867-4900 🚌 15, 57, 110, 160

Staff are able to help with bookings

MANSIÓN VITRAUX $$$

www.mansionvitraux.com

A stone's throw from San Telmo's Plaza Dorrego, this small and beautiful hotel offers a wide range of facilities and services, from hypoallergenic pillows to wine tasting in the cellar, which doubles as a contemporary breakfast room.

🔢 H9 ✉ Carlos Calvo 369 ☎ 4300-6886 🚌 10, 22, 29, 126

MILHOUSE $

www.milhousehostel.com

Housed in two 19th-century mansions on the iconic Avenida de Mayo, the excellent Milhouse youth hostel prides itself on offering non-stop entertainment in the shape of salsa and tango lessons, walking tours and visits to football and polo matches.

🔢 F7 ✉ Hipólito Yrigoyen 959 ☎ 4383-9383 🚇 Avenida de Mayo

MINE $$

www.minehotel.com

Mine has made a name for its professional, friendly service and fashionable style, with DVD players in every room and an excellent, healthy breakfast served in the airy café or on the bijou patio. It is in Palermo—where else?

🔢 A5 ✉ Gorriti 4770 ☎ 4832-1100 🚌 15, 55, 168

MORENO $$

www.morenobuenosaires.com

As if the 39 capacious rooms and lofts, all sleek lines and mod cons, were not enough, this original San Telmo hotel features a theatre and tango lounge and a restaurant famed for its inventive cuisine. Eco-friendly, the hotel also offers a carbon-offsetting programme.

➕ H8 ✉ Moreno 376 ☎ 6091-2000
🚇 Bolívar 🚌 29, 56

OSTINATTO $

www.ostinatto.com

This stunning 1920s building in San Telmo has been brought into the 21st century with minimalist sleekness. The white-and-red colour scheme is enhanced by light from the glass roof. Regular Spanish classes are given on-site.

➕ G8 ✉ Chile 680 ☎ 4362-9639
🚇 Belgrano

POSADA DE LA LUNA $

www.posadaluna.com

You must stay at least two nights at this downtown *posada* five blocks from the Plaza de Mayo, but that should not pose a problem. The spacious rooms with beautiful wooden floors and bright decor are a real pleasure.

➕ G8 ✉ Perú 565 ☎ 4361-0737
🚇 Belgrano

RIBERA SUR $$

www.riberasurhotel.com.ar

In an unusual location on the edge of San Telmo, Ribera Sur has 16 cozy but functional rooms where the decor is lifted by colourful details such as artesanal throws. There is an excellent restaurant next to the heated pool and deck.

➕ H9 ✉ Avenida Paseo Colón 1145
☎ 4361-7398 🚌 93, 152

ROONEY'S $$

www.rooneysboutiquehotel.com

This stylish downtown hotel is arranged around a lounge bar, patio and café. There is an old-world charm about this welcoming and utterly comfortable hotel that lays on free tango lessons.

➕ E7 ✉ Sarmiento 1775 3rd floor
☎ 5252-5060 🚇 Callao (B) 🚌 12, 37, 124

TAILOR MADE HOTEL $$

www.tailormadehotels.com

The term tailor-made is sometimes emptily bandied about but in the case of this exquisite Las Cañitas hotel, with its five rooms, it is totally appropriate. The rates include free international phone calls, bike rental, WiFi, laundry and snacks and drinks.

➕ I13 ✉ Arce 385 ☎ 4774-9620
🚇 Ministro Carranza (D) 🚌 15, 60, 152, 160

ULTRA $$

www.hotelultra.com

A couple of blocks from Palermo's trendy Plaza Serrano, the Ultra lives up to its name: ultra comfortable with its enticing decor and lie-back-and-relax bath-tubs; ultra trendy with its postmodern bistro; and ultra exclusive with only 20 rooms, each with special details.

➕ A4 ✉ Gorriti 4929 ☎ 4833-9200
🚌 15, 55, 57, 140

SLEEP

Need to Know

This section takes you through all the practical aspects of your trip to make it run more smoothly and to give you confidence before you go and while you are there.

NEED TO KNOW

Planning Ahead

WHEN TO GO

Buenos Aires has a subtropical climate, with hot, humid summers and cool, damp winters. The best time to visit is spring, when there is plenty going on, the weather is bright and the trees are in bloom, though autumn is pleasant, too. Peak holiday times are January, Easter and early July.

TIME

Buenos Aires is 3 hours behind GMT and 2 hours ahead of New York.

TEMPERATURE

JAN	FEB	MAR	APR	MAY	JUN	JUL	AUG	SEP	OCT	NOV	DEC
87°F	84°F	80°F	73°F	66°F	60°F	59°F	63°F	66°F	73°F	78°F	81°F
30°C	29°C	26°C	23°C	19°C	16°C	15°C	17°C	19°C	23°C	25°C	27°C

Spring (late September to early December) is warm and sunny though showers are to be expected.

Summer (mid-December to early March) can get very sticky but frequent storms clear the air.

Autumn (mid-March to early June) sees temperatures drop off along with the humidity and intense blue skies are not uncommon.

Winter (mid-June to early September) alternates between grey mist and azure skies with brilliant sunshine—frost is virtually unheard of. July is the driest month of the year on average.

WHAT'S ON

January/February *Chinese New Year*: China Town (Barrio Chino) celebrates with processions.

February *Copa Claro*: Men's open tennis championships at the Lawn Tennis Club in Palermo.

March *Buenos Aires Fashion (BAF)*: Autumn and winter collections.

April *Buenos Aires Festival Internacional de Cine Independiente*: Hoyts Abasto cinema hosts the city's indie film festival.

May *25 de Mayo*: Independence celebrations on the Plaza de Mayo.
arteBA: Buenos Aires' annual contemporary art fair at La Rural.

June *Ciudad Emergente*: Government-run festival that showcases up-and-coming artists.

July *Exposición de Ganadería*: A huge exhibition of livestock and gauchos at the Predio La Rural in Palermo.
9 de Julio: The national holiday celebrations are low key with lots of hot chocolate on a cold day (it even snowed in 2007!).

August *Festival y Mundial del Tango*: A major national and international tango festival.

September *Feria de Vinos y Bodegas*: Palermo's Predio La Rural hosts a wine fair.

October *Maratón Internacional de Buenos Aires*: Spring is the ideal time for this road race.
Casa Foa: Window into the latest in Argentine design—the venue and date change every year.

November *Día de la Tradición*: 10 November is set aside for celebrating *criollo* culture.

December *Buenos Aires Jazz Festival Internacional*: Tango and rock give way to jazz at various venues.

BUENOS AIRES ONLINE

www.buenosairesherald.com
Argentina's leading English-language daily is a mine of information—its motto is 'a world of information in a few words'. It carries cultural events of interest to English speakers plus listings of art galleries and the like.

www.buenosairestimes.com
A bilingual English-Spanish site with lots of up-to-date information aimed at tourists, with hotel reviews and some useful general info.

www.buenosairesturismo.com.ar
This unofficial site has loads of information on accommodation, climate, events, attractions, sport, tango and health-related tourism.

www.lanacion.com.ar
It's in Spanish only, but the website of Argentina's most prestigious broadsheet is easy to navigate and includes excellent sections on cultural events.

www.saexplorers.org
South American Explorers offers independent information and advice. Their chain of welcoming clubhouses across the continent includes one in the Argentine capital.

www.thegayguide.com.ar
This comprehensive guide has information on clubs, bars, gay-friendly restaurants and cafés.

www.viajaracolonia.com.ar
Colonia del Sacramento in Uruguay is worth at least a day trip by ferry. This site will help you to find out about this colonial town.

www.welcomeargentina.com
An extremely useful website with links and addresses for accommodation and places to eat, tour agencies and monuments.

www.whatsupbuenosaires.com
Easily the best English-language website for cultural events.

USEFUL TRAVEL SITES

www.theAA.com
www.fodors.com
www.bue.gov.ar
Excellent official Buenos Aires' site, with all manner of information.
www.ohbuenosaires.com
Multilingual site with highly useful facts about every aspect of the city.

INTERNET CAFÉS

● In most of the *barrios* you will find dozens of *locutorios* (public communications centres) and kiosks with at least two or three computers with internet access, in addition to telephone cabins. One exception is Palermo Viejo, where they are few and far between.
● WiFi access is common in hotels, restaurants, cafés and public places—look for the sign and if need be ask for the password *(contraseña)*.

Getting There

ENTRY REQUIREMENTS

● Citizens of Australia, Canada, Ireland, New Zealand, South Africa, the UK, the US and all European countries need a valid passport to enter Argentina but not a visa.

● A landing form *(tarjeta de entrada)* must be filled in and presented with your passport when you go through ID controls upon entry; these forms are usually provided by cabin crew on flights. Remember to sign it.

● Another form has to be filled in when you leave—you are given one when you check in at the point of departure.

● Your passport will be stamped on entry (and departure) and you will normally be given 90 days to stay in the country.

● Australian, Canadian and US passport-holders must pay a reciprocity fee upon entry; check for details before you travel.

TRAVEL BETWEEN AIRPORTS

Manuel Tienda León (www.tiendaleon.com.ar) runs a useful, albeit infrequent service, between Aeroparque and Ezeiza, which can help if you have a domestic connection immediately upon arrival. It charges $50.

AIRPORTS

Ezeiza (Ministro Pistarini) is where international flights arrive and depart, with the exception of all flights to and from Uruguay and some serving Santiago (Chile) and São Paulo (Brazil) which use Aeroparque.

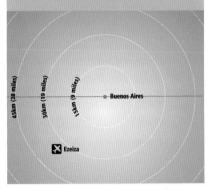

FROM EZEIZA

Ministro Pistarini, the international airport, is better known as Ezeiza (EZE), the small town where it is located, 35km (22 miles) southwest of Buenos Aires. The flight from London (with stopover) takes about 16 hours; from New York it takes 11 hours non-stop.

The quickest and most convenient way to the city centre is by *remise* (radio cab). Several companies have offices in the arrivals hall, as you emerge from customs. The main *remise* companies are Manuel Tienda León (tel 4315-5115; www.tiendaleon.com.ar) and Transfer Express (tel 4312-8883). Compare prices and availability before choosing. The journey time is about 50 minutes, though traffic and weather conditions mean it could take longer. The cost is around $150, including all luggage and the motorway tolls and you can pay by credit card. After paying (keep the receipt), wait by the office for your driver to escort you to the car. You will need the exact destination address.

Manuel Tienda León also runs a minibus service at regular set times throughout the day, at least twice an hour. It costs $45 for the one-way transfer to its main office at Terminal Madero in Retiro, but add a drop-off service to most addresses within the city centre. A large number of the city's hostels offer a similar service, which must be booked in advance online at www.hostelshuttle.com.ar. Services start at 8am, with five departures throughout the day until 6.30. The journey time is around 75 minutes; the cost is $14.

You could also take a city taxi but make sure you pay in advance at the official taxi desk in the arrivals hall. You tell them the destination and pay a fixed fare, which should be no more than $100.

There is a bus (No. 60), which for $1.50 will eventually get you to the Avenida de Mayo.

FROM AEROPARQUE
Flights to and from Uruguay and some to Chile and Brazil, along with most internal connections, use the domestic airport, Aeroparque Metropolitano Jorge Newbery (known as Aeroparque), only 6km (4 miles) north of Buenos Aires at Palermo's Costanera Norte. A few domestic flights depart from Ezeiza, however, so check well in advance.

Plentiful taxis filter through a rank by arrivals at busy peak times and will get you to Palermo quickly (under $20), and other *barrios* in less than 30 minutes in good traffic for $20–$40.

Manuel Tienda León has *remises* that get you to your destination for $20–$50 depending on the distance; you have to wait a while but the cars are good and there is usually more room for luggage than in a standard taxi.

A regular minibus service by Manuel Tienda León runs all day between Aeroparque and its Madero terminus costing $17 one way. If that sounds too expensive, bus No. 33 passes the arrivals exit and terminates on the Paseo Colón on the riverside downtown.

- There is no reciprocal health agreement between Argentina and most other countries, so a fully comprehensive insurance is vital. You might need to contact your company for clearance before treatment.
- Health services are good but you should be aware of the effects of phenomena such as high temperatures or strong sunshine on anyone with vulnerabilities, such as heart ailments.
- If you have any treatment, make sure you get a proper invoice so that you can claim from your insurance company. This might cover items like dental treatment, eye-tests and medical check-ups, all of which are much less expensive than in most industrialized nations.

CUSTOMS

- Adult visitors from most countries may import duty-free: 400 cigarettes, 2 litres of alcoholic drinks; 5kg (11lb) of foodstuffs and 100ml of perfume.
- Restricted items for import include certain animal products including milk and fruit and flowers.

Getting Around

NEED TO KNOW

DRIVING

With affordable taxis, an extensive public transportation system and chaotic streets, you are advised not to drive while in Buenos Aires. Gridlocks and unruly drivers, restricted parking and expensive car parks are additional reasons not to get behind a wheel. If you do decide to rent a car, be prepared for a stressful time and familiarize yourself with some local rules of the road. The lower age limit for car rental is between 21 and 25.

● You may be fined for violating the highway code (*código vial*) and some of the rules may differ from those in your home country.

● You must drive on the right and overtake on the left.

● You should give way to traffic coming from the right unless you are on a major highway or the road sign says otherwise.

GUIDED TOURS

Buenos Aires Tur
www.buenosairestur.com
Very reliable company offering a range of tours in and around the city

Tangol
www.tangol.com
Tours from tango to gaucho days out

Tourist Bus
www.bue.gov.ar
A new double-decker bus with fixed hop-on-and-off city tours run by the municipality

THE SUBTE

Buenos Aires' metro service, *subte* (*subterráneo*), run privately by Metrovías, is one of the oldest (1913) but is neither the most convenient nor the most comfortable in the world. However, it can be useful for getting quickly to certain destinations.

There are six lines: A, the oldest and most picturesque, running from Plaza de Mayo along Avenida de Mayo to the western *barrios*; B from the downtown riverside to the northwestern *barrios*; C connecting the Retiro railway station to another major commuter hub at Constitución; D from Plaza de Mayo to Palermo and Belgrano; E from Plaza de Mayo to the southwestern *barrios*; and new H from Once to the southern *barrios*. Each line is colour coded on maps and at stations.

● There is a regular service from 5am to 10.30pm every day of the year, though wildcat industrial action is not infrequent.

● Trains are frequent (around five to ten an hour) but can get very crowded at peak hours—7.30 to 9am and 5.30 to 7pm.

● Tickets cost $1.10. You can buy the magnetic paper tickets several at a time or one SubtePass ticket for several journeys (*viajes*).

● You might also obtain a contactless Monedero card. These can be recharged with cash but are only worth getting if you plan to use the *subte* a lot.

● Put your ticket through the slot by the barriers and hold on to it, especially if it has remaining journeys; you do not need it to leave the station, though.

● A number of station walls are decorated with beautiful murals or decorative tiles.

● The Belgian-built wooden rolling-stock still used on Línea A is up to 70 years old and is a tourist attraction in itself.

BUSES

Known as *colectivos*, or colloquially as *bondis*, the city's privately run single-decker buses are noisy and fast, but there are lots of them.

Bus stops *(paradas)* are marked by discreet dark blue signs atop posts on the pavement (sidewalk), which show the route number and terminus plus some main stops along the route. Don't expect to see any shelters, route maps or timetables.

● On most routes the frequency varies from four to seven buses an hour.

● If you can work out the route you need, hop on and tell the driver *(colectivero)* where you are going—preferably a street intersection. Don't expect much help but s/he should say how much you need to slot in the machine for your ticket *(boleto)*, usually around $1.10.

● It is worth investing in a copy of *Guía T*. This cheap booklet sold at all kiosks contains page-by-page city maps with all the bus routes.

● There is no night bus service as such but many routes are served 24/7 (e.g. 5 and 86).

TRAMS

Apart from the touristy Tranvía Histórico in outlying Caballito, there is only one tram in Buenos Aires, the Tranvía del Este running parallel to Puerto Madero. Since 2007 this bright yellow tram has slid up and down renovated tracks between the northern end of Dique 4 and the southern end of Dique 2.

TAXIS

Buenos Aires taxis are black and yellow and there are loads of them—usually you can easily find one to hail anywhere in the centre, even late at night. There are ranks at airports, stations and bus terminals. A red LIBRE light means the cab is free for hire. Make sure the driver switches the meter on. Fares are relatively low and it is customary to round up to the nearest $0.50 or peso, but tips are not expected. Drivers will not accept large notes (unless the fare is particularly high).

● For longer journeys, such as to Ezeiza, or in certain *barrios* it may be better to call for a radio cab *(remise)*.
Ciudad tel 011/4923-7444
Premium tel 011/4374-6666
Tres Sargentos tel 011/4312-0057

Social awareness and concerted efforts by the authorities have greatly improved conditions for the disabled *(discapacitados)*, but there is still a long way to go. People are extremely helpful and there will usually be volunteers to help lift wheelchairs or give assistance. If you are disabled you should try to travel with at least one person who can help you to get around.

● Make sure you have everything you need, such as wheelchair spare parts. Wheelchairs are provided at most Argentine airports—it is best to call ahead to let them know your needs. Check-in staff and ground crews are usually helpful.

● Most taxis are not suitable for people with disabilities nor can they store wheelchairs in the boot (trunk) —call a radio taxi *(remise)* company and ask for a special vehicle.

● Some buses have wheelchair access.

● Many new hotels have special rooms that are adapted to the disabled, but standards may not be what you are used to at home.

● Dogs are welcome almost everywhere so guide dogs are unlikely to be refused.

● Pavements (sidewalks) are often in a poor state and ramps at street corners can be rickety.

Essential Facts

ETIQUETTE

● Dress is informal but smart—too much bare flesh at the wrong time and place is frowned upon. Dressing up is appreciated in top hotels and chic restaurants.

● Smoking is illegal on public transportation, in public buildings and in all enclosed places where food is served.

● Tipping is not compulsory, though in touristy cafés and restaurants wait staff might expect a gratuity of 5–10 per cent. Taxi drivers do not expect a tip; hotel porters do.

EMBASSIES

● **Australia** ✉ Villanueva 1400, Buenos Aires 1426 ☎ 011/4777-6580; www.argentina.embassy.gov.au
● **Canada** ✉ Tagle 2828, Buenos Aires 1425 ☎ 011/4805-3032; www.buenosaires.gc.ca
● **Ireland** ✉ Avenida del Libertador 1068, Piso 6, Buenos Aires 1112 ☎ 011/5787-0801; www.embassyofireland.org.ar
● **New Zealand** ✉ Avenida Corrientes 456, Piso 6, Buenos Aires 1011 ☎ 011/4328-0747; www.nzembassy.com/buenosaires
● **UK** ✉ Dr. Luis Agote 2412, Buenos Aires 1425 ☎ 011/4803-7070; www.britain.org.ar
● **US** ✉ Avenida Colombia 4300 Buenos Aires 1425 ☎ 011/4777-4533; www.argentina.usembassy.gov

ELECTRICITY

● Electricity is 220 volts and 50 Hertz. The sockets are of two sorts: two-pin, with a slightly thicker pin than the European two-pin plugs; and three-pin, with flat pins in a triangular format. Both usually take European two-pin plugs but neither accepts any other type of plugs, so you will need an adaptor.

● North American visitors will also need a transformer to cope with the different voltage.

MEDICAL TREATMENT

● There are many good clinics or health centres *(clínicas* or *centros medicos)*—try Swiss Medical (www.swissmedical.com.ar) for good quality and English-speaking staff.

● Staff at pharmacies *(farmacias)* can give advice for basic problems.

● Ask your hotel to call for a doctor *(médico)*; most will speak some English.

MEDICINES

● It is worth getting a repeat prescription for vital medicines before you travel—or note the pharmaceutical name of your drugs, as the local brand name might be different.

MONEY MATTERS

● Argentina's inflation rate has been as high as 25 per cent, so check currency exchange rates before you travel.

● The $ sign is used for pesos—US dollars are shown as US$ or USD, though always check to make sure. A dollar is worth about 4 pesos.

● Travellers' cheques are fairly hard to change and cannot be used as cash. Keep some cash with you as not everywhere takes credit cards.

● ATMs *(cajeros automáticos)* are plentiful and accept most international debit and credit cards (it is best to check before travelling); the machines have English-language choices. Most allow you to take out a maximum of $700 (pesos) in each transaction, so you may have to repeat the withdrawal several times to reach your own bank limit.

● Banks *(bancos)* are numerous and many belong to international chains. It is usually advantageous to change money in bureaux de change as the commission is lower.

● Banking hours are usually Mon–Fri 10–4.

● There are many exchange bureaux (cámbios) in downtown and their opening hours are much longer than for banks. You will need your passport to change money.

● All the major credit cards (tarjetas de crédito) are widely accepted, except in small shops. If staying at an estancia (▷ 159, panel), establish first whether they take plastic.

● You rarely need to enter a PIN when using credit cards for purchases but you might be asked for ID to check your signature. Keep a note of card details in case of loss or theft.

MAIL AND TELEPHONES

● Post office opening hours are 9–6 on weekdays and 9–1 on Saturdays. Postal rates are high and the service is slow and unreliable. It is best to use courier services instead.

● Stamps (estampillas) are sold at post offices (correos) and occasionally at hotels and shops selling postcards. The rates for international mail are very high.

● Letter boxes are often British-style pillar-boxes, but it is safer to hand in mail to the post office for dispatch.

● Telephones work fairly well but the rates, especially for inter-regional and international calls, are high—check out discount cards.

● Buy prepaid phone cards at kiosks, public call centres and Pharmacity drugstores. Called Hablemás and Colibrí, they cost $3.50. You must dial a given telephone number, depending on where you are, and then enter a number revealed by scratching the card. These cards reduce the cost of calling abroad.

● Avoid using the telephone in your hotel room as rates are high.

● There are few public telephones; instead everyone uses public call centres (locutorios), which often double up as internet centres. Make sure you have change to pay for calls—large notes are not accepted.

● To call overseas dial 00 then the country code and the number (minus initial 0).

Words and Phrases

Spanish is phonetic and particular combinations of letters are always pronounced the same way. When a word ends in a vowel, 'n' or 's', the stress is usually on the penultimate syllable; otherwise, it falls on the last syllable. Note that 'll' and 'y' sound like the 's' in treasure, and not lisping 'z' or 'c'. A major difference from Spanish in Spain is the use of vos instead of tú (informal 'you').

RESTAURANT

I'd like to reserve a table for ... people at...
Quisiera reservar una mesa para ... personas para las...
A table for ... please
Una mesa para ... por favor
Could we sit here?
¿Nos podemos sentar acá?
Waiter/waitress
El mozo/la moza
Where are the toilets?
¿Dónde están los baños?
Could we see the menu/ wine list?
¿Podemos ver la carta/ carta de vinos?
I can't eat wheat/sugar/salt/ dairy/nuts
No puedo comer trigo/azúcar/ cerdo/productos lácteos/ frutos secos
I ordered...
Yo pedí...
I'd like...
Quisiera...
May I have the bill, please?
¿La cuenta, por favor?
Is service included?
¿Está incluido el servicio?
The bill (check) is not right
La cuenta no está correcta
I'd like to speak to the manager
Quiero hablar con el encargado
knife/fork/spoon
el cuchillo/el tenedor/ la cuchara

CONVERSATION

What is the time? — *¿Qué hora es?*
I don't speak Spanish — *No hablo castellano*
Do you speak English? — *¿Habla inglés?*
I don't understand — *No entiendo*
Please repeat that — *Por favor repita eso*
Please speak more slowly — *Por favor hable más despacio*
Can you write that for me? — *¿Me lo puede escribir?*
What does this mean? — *¿Qué significa esto?*
Good morning/afternoon — *Buen día/buenas tardes*
Good evening/night — *Buenas noches*
Goodbye — *Adiós/chau*
That's all right — *Está bien*
I don't know — *No lo sé*
Don't mention it — *De nada*

GETTING AROUND

Where is the information desk? — *¿Dónde está el mostrador de información?*
Does this train/bus go to ...? — *¿Va este tren/colectivo a ...?*
Does this train/bus stop at ...? — *¿Para este tren/colectivo en ...?*
Can I have a one-way/ return ticket to ...? — *¿Me da un billete sencillo/ de ida y vuelta para...?*
Where are we? — *¿Dónde estamos?*
I'm lost — *Estoy perdido*
Is this the way to ...? — *¿Es éste el camino para ir a ...?*
Where can I find a taxi? — *¿Dónde puedo encontrar un taxi?*
Please take me to ... — *A .... por favor*
Can you turn on the meter, please? — *¿Baje la bandera, por favor?*

USEFUL WORDS

yes	*sí*
no	*non*
please	*por favor*
thank you	*gracias*
there	*allí*
where	*dónde*
here	*acá*
when	*cuándo*
I'm sorry	*Lo siento*
Excuse me	*permiso*

EMERGENCIES/HEALTH

Help!	*Socorro*
Stop thief!	*Al ladrón*
I have lost my passport/ wallet/purse/bag	*Perdí el pasaporte/la billetera/el monedero/ la cartera*
I have had an accident	*Tuve un incidente*
I have been robbed	*Me han robado*
Where is the police station?	*¿Dónde está la comisaría?*
Could you call a doctor?	*¿Puede llamar a un médico?*
Hospital	*El hospital*
I need to see a doctor/ dentist	*Necesito un médico/ dentista*

ACCOMMODATION

Do you have a room?	*¿Tiene una habitación?*
I have a reservation for ... nights	*Tengo una reserva para ... noches*
Double room with double bed	*Habitación doble con cama matrimonial*
Single room	*Habitación single*
Twin room	*Habitación twin*
With bath/shower	*Con bañera/ducha*
Air conditioning	*Aire acondicionado*
Non-smoking	*No fumador*
Is breakfast included?	*¿Está el desayuno incluido?*
When is breakfast served?	*¿A qué hora se sirve el desayuno?*
Is there a lift (elevator)?	*¿Hay ascensor?*

NUMBERS

1	*uno*
2	*dos*
3	*tres*
4	*cuatro*
5	*cinco*
6	*seis*
7	*siete*
8	*ocho*
9	*nueve*
10	*diez*
11	*once*
12	*doce*
13	*trece*
14	*catorce*
15	*quince*
16	*dieciséis*
17	*diecisiete*
18	*dieciocho*
19	*diecinueve*
20	*veinte*
100	*cien*
1,000	*mil*

TIMES AND DAYS

Monday	*lunes*
Tuesday	*martes*
Wednesday	*miércoles*
Thursday	*jueves*
Friday	*viernes*
Saturday	*sábado*
Sunday	*domingo*
morning	*la mañana*
afternoon	*la tarde*
evening	*la tarde/noche*
day	*el día*
night	*la noche*
today	*hoy (en día)*
yesterday	*ayer*
tomorrow	*mañana*
now	*ahora*
later	*más tarde*

Index

The Automobile Association would like to thank the following photographers, companies and picture libraries for their assistance in the preparation of this book.

Abbreviations for the picture credits are as follows – (t) top; (b) bottom; (c) centre; (l) left; (r) right; (AA) AA World Travel Library.

2t AA/Y Levy; **2tc** AA/Y Levy; **2c** AA/Y Levy; **2bc** AA/Y Levy; **2b** AA/Y Levy; **3t** AA/Y Levy; **3tc** AA/Y Levy; **3bc** AA/Y Levy; **3b** AA/Y Levy; **4** AA/Y Levy; **5** AA/Y Levy; **6/7t** AA/Y Levy; **6/7tc** AA/Y Levy; **6/7bc** AA/Y Levy; **6/7b** AA/Y Levy; **7t** AA/Y Levy; **7b** AA/Y Levy; **8t** AA/Y Levy; **8b** AA/Y Levy; **8/9t** AA/Y Levy; **8/9c** AA/Y Levy; **8/9b** AA/Y Levy; **10l** AGIP/Rue des Archives/Mary Evans; **10r** AA/Y Levy; **11** AA/Y Levy; **12** AA/Y Levy; **14l** AA/Y Levy; **14r** AA/Y Levy; **14/5** AA/Y Levy; **15l** AA/Y Levy; **15r** AA/Y Levy; **15b** AA/Y Levy; **16t** AA/Y Levy; **16b** AA/Y Levy; **16/7** AA/Y Levy; **17l** AA/Y Levy; **17r** AA/Y Levy; **18** AA/Y Levy; **18/9t** AA/Y Levy; **18/9b** AA/Y Levy; **19t** AA/Y Levy; **19b** AA/Y Levy; **20** AA/Y Levy; **20/1t** AA/Y Levy; **20/1b** AA/Y Levy; **21t** AA/Y Levy; **21B** AA/Y Levy; **22** AA/Y Levy; **23t** AA/Y Levy; **23b** AA/Y Levy; **24l** AA/Y Levy; **24r** AA/Y Levy; **24/5** AA/Y Levy; **25l** AA/Y Levy; **25r** AA/Y Levy; **25b** AA/Y Levy; **26t** AA/Y Levy; **26b** AA/Y Levy; **26/7t** AA/Y Levy; **26/7b** AA/Y Levy; **27b** AA/Y Levy; **28l** AA/Y Levy; **28r** AA/Y Levy; **28/9** AA/Y Levy; **29l** AA/Y Levy; **29r** AA/Y Levy; **30** AA/Y Levy; **30/1t** AA/Y Levy; **30/1b** AA/Y Levy; **31t** AA/Y Levy; **31b** AA/Y Levy; **32/3** AA/Y Levy; **33** AA/Y Levy; **34** AA/Y Levy; **34/5t** AA/Y Levy; **34/5b** AA/Y Levy; **35** AA/Y Levy; **36** AA/Y Levy; **36/7** AA/Y Levy; **37t** AA/Y Levy; **37b** AA/Y Levy; **38** AA/Y Levy; **38/9t** AA/Y Levy; **38/9b** AA/Y Levy; **39t** AA/Y Levy; **39B** AA/Y Levy; **40/1** © Walter Bibikow/JAI/Corbis; **41** Photolibrary; **42/3** AA/Y Levy; **43** AA/Y Levy; **44** AA/Y Levy; **44/5b** AA/Y Levy; **45** AA/Y Levy; **46t** AA/Y Levy; **46b** AA/Y Levy; **46/7b** AA/Y Levy; **47tl** AA/Y Levy; **47tr** AA/Y Levy; **47b** AA/Y Levy; **48** AA/Y Levy; **48/9t** AA/Y Levy; **48/9b** AA/Y Levy; **49** AA/Y Levy; **50/1** AA/Y Levy; **51** AA/Y Levy; **52l** AA/Y Levy; **52r** AA/Y Levy; **52/3** AA/Y Levy; **53tl** AA/Y Levy; **53tr** AA/Y Levy; **53b** AA/Y Levy; **54** AA/Y Levy; **54/5t** AA/Y Levy; **54/5b** AA/Y Levy; **55** AA/Y Levy; **56l** AA/Y Levy; **56r** AA/Y Levy; **56/7** AA/Y Levy; **57tl** AA/Y Levy; **57tr** AA/Y Levy; **57b** AA/Y Levy; **58/9** © Peter Horree/Alamy; **59** AA/Y Levy; **60** AA/Y Levy; **60/1** AA/Y Levy; **61t** AA/Y Levy; **61b** AA/Y Levy; **62** AA/Y Levy; **62/3t** AA/Y Levy; **62/3b** AA/Y Levy; **63t** AA/Y Levy; **63b** AA/Y Levy; **64** AA/Y Levy; **66l** AA/Y Levy; **66r** AA/Y Levy; **67l** AA/Y Levy; **67r** AA/Y Levy; **68** AA/Y Levy; **69l** AA/Y Levy; **69r** AA/Y Levy; **70l** AA/Y Levy; **70r** AA/Y Levy; **71** © Bernardo Galmarini/Alamy; **72l** AA/Y Levy; **72r** AA/Y Levy; **73** AA/Y Levy; **74** AA/Y Levy; **75l** AA/Y Levy; **75r** AA/Y Levy; **76l** AA/Y Levy; **76r** AA/Y Levy; **77** AA/Y Levy; **78** AA/Y Levy; **80** AA/Y Levy; **81l** AA/Y Levy; **81r** AA/Y Levy; **84(I)** AA/Y Levy; **84(II)** AA/Y Levy; **84(III)** AA/Y Levy; **84(IV)** AA/Y Levy; **84(V)** AA/Y Levy; **84(VI)** AA/Y Levy; **86** AA/Y Levy; **87t** AA/Y Levy; **87b** AA/Y Levy; **90t** AA/Y Levy; **90tc** AA/Y Levy; **90C** AA/Y Levy; **90bc** AA/Y Levy; **90b** AA/Y Levy; **92t** AA/Y Levy; **92b** AA/Y Levy; **93t** AA/Y Levy; **93b** AA/Y Levy; **96t** AA/Y Levy; **96tc** AA/Y Levy; **96c** AA/Y Levy; **96bc** AA/Y Levy; **96b** AA/Y Levy; **98t** AA/Y Levy; **98b** AA/Y Levy; **99t** AA/Y Levy; **99b** AA/Y Levy; **102(I)** AA/Y Levy; **102(II)** AA/Y Levy; **102(III)** AA/Y Levy; **102(IV)** AA/Y Levy; **102(V)** AA/Y Levy; **102(VI)** AA/Y Levy; **104** AA/Y Levy; **105** AA/Y Levy; **108t** AA/Y Levy; **108b** AA/Y Levy; **109** © Bernardo Galmarini/Alamy; **110t** AA/Y Levy; **110b** AA/Y Levy; **111t** AA/Y Levy; **111b** AA/Y Levy; **114** AA/Y Levy; **115** Photolibrary; **116** AA/Y Levy; **118** AA/Y Levy; **118/9t** AA/Y Levy; **118/9tc** AA/Y Levy; **118/9bc** AA/Y Levy; **118/9b** AA/Y Levy; **119** AA/Y Levy; **123** AA/Y Levy; **127** AA/Y Levy; **128** AA/Y Levy; **130/1t** AA/Y Levy; **130/1tc** AA/Y Levy; **130/1bc** AA/Y Levy; **130/1b** AA/Y Levy; **131t** AA/Y Levy; **131b** AA/Y Levy; **133** AA/Y Levy; **135** AA/Y Levy; **136** AA/Y Levy; **138** AA/Y Levy; **140t** AA/Y Levy; **140tc** AA/Y Levy; **140bc** AA/Y Levy; **140b** AA/Y Levy; **143** AA/Y Levy; **146** AA/Y Levy; **149l** AA/Y Levy; **149r** AA/Y Levy; **152** AA/Y Levy; **154t** AA/Y Levy; **154tc** AA/Y Levy; **154bc** AA/Y Levy; **154b** AA/Y Levy; **157l** AA/Y Levy; **157r** AA/Y Levy; **158** AA/Y Levy; **160** AA/Y Levy.

Every effort has been made to trace the copyright holders, and we apologise in advance for any unintentional omissions or errors. We would be pleased to apply any corrections in a following edition of this publication.

CITYPACK TOP 25
Buenos Aires

WRITTEN BY Andrew Benson
VERIFIED BY Matt Chesterton
COVER DESIGN Nick Johnston
DESIGN WORK Tracey Butler
INDEXER Marie Lorimer
IMAGE RETOUCHING AND REPRO Jacqueline Street
PROJECT EDITOR Bookwork Creative Ltd
SERIES EDITOR Marie-Claire Jefferies

© **AA MEDIA LIMITED 2012**

First published 2012

Colour separation by AA Digital Department
Printed and bound by Leo Paper Products, China

A CIP catalogue record for this book is available from the British Library.

ISBN 978-0-7495-7088-0

The content of this book is believed to be accurate at the time of printing. Due to its nature the content is likely to vary or change and the publisher is not responsible for such change and accordingly is not responsible for the consequences of any reliance by the reader on information that has changed. Any rights that are given to consumers under applicable law are not affected. Opinions expressed are for guidance only and are those of the assessor based on their experience at the time of review and may differ from the reader's opinions based on their subsequent experience.

We have tried to ensure accuracy in this guide, but things do change, so please let us know if you have any comments at travelguides@theAA.com.

Published by AA Publishing, a trading name of AA Media Limited, whose registered office is Fanum House, Basing View, Basingstoke, Hampshire RG21 4EA. Registered number 06112600.

A03997
Maps in this title produced from map data supplied by Global Mapping, Brackley, UK © Global Mapping/ITMB
Transport map © Communicarta Ltd, UK